ICFA Continuing Education
Managing Asset/Liability Portfolios

December 4, 1991
New York, New York

David F. Babbel
H. Gifford Fong
Jack L. Gibson
Martin L. Leibowitz
Robert J. Matczak

Josie McElhone
Thomas E. Messmore, CFA
Phillip D. Parker
Alfred Weinberger
Eliot P. Williams, CFA, *Moderator*

Edited by Eliot P. Williams, CFA

To obtain an AIMR Publications Catalog or to order additional copies of this publication, turn to page 71 or contact:

AIMR Publications Sales Department
P.O. Box 7947
Charlottesville, VA 22906
Telephone: 804/980-3647
Fax: 804/977-0350

The Association for Investment Management and Research comprises the Institute of Chartered Financial Analysts and the Financial Analysts Federation.

ISBN 1-879087-16-2

Printed in the United States of America

6/15/92

Table of Contents

Foreword

As the result of the financial challenges that arose during the 1980s, many financial institutions began to focus on better definitions and more precise monitoring of the risks associated with both assets and liabilities. It soon became clear that asset allocations that are optimal in an assets-only framework are not optimal when liabilities are considered. Increasingly, the objective function is being recognized as the management of surplus—which can be defined as the difference between the current value of assets and the present value of liabilities—rather than the management of assets alone.

Asset allocation for asset/liability portfolios is a more complex problem than for assets-only situations, primarily because liabilities themselves are complex. Their special constraints can lead to solutions that are different from the market-optimal allocations. Many difficulties arise from the fact that we do not have market value accounting. Others relate to the fact that many liabilities possess embedded options. New approaches to allocation incorporate liabilities as a negative asset class and take into account constraints, business flows, and factor sensitivities in developing optimal asset mix combinations.

Much of the asset/liability literature does not address the real-world considerations portfolio managers must contend with in managing the assets of financial institutions. The proceedings that follows has been designed to (1) review a host of recent developments in this dynamic area, (2) summarize and discuss their interconnections, and (3) provide one forum in which theory and practice can come together in a way that is useful to practitioners.

Although many people contributed to the success of the seminar and this proceedings, special thanks are due to Eliot P. Williams, CFA. As editor of the proceedings as well as conference moderator, his wisdom permeates this publication. We appreciate his time and effort.

The speakers contributing to the seminar were David F. Babbel, Wharton School, University of Pennsylvania; H. Gifford Fong, Gifford Fong Associates; Jack L. Gibson, Coopers & Lybrand; Martin L. Leibowitz, Salomon Brothers, Inc.; Robert J. Matczak, Coopers & Lybrand; Josie McElhone, Home Federal Loan Mortgage Corporation; Thomas E. Messmore, CFA, the Travelers Insurance Company; Phillip D. Parker, Securities and Exchange Commission; Alfred Weinberger, Salomon Brothers; and Eliot P. Williams, CFA, the Travelers Insurance Company.

Katrina F. Sherrerd, CFA
Vice President
Publications and Research
AIMR

Biographies of Speakers

David F. Babbel is an associate professor at the Wharton School, University of Pennsylvania. He teaches in the graduate program, primarily in the areas of investments, insurance finance, and corporate finance. Prior to joining the university faculty, Mr. Babbel taught at the University of California at Berkeley for seven years, principally in the areas of international financial management and investments. A former vice president and director of research in the Pension and Insurance Department at Goldman, Sachs & Co., Mr. Babbel has been a financial consultant for 15 large national and international organizations. He is coauthor of a textbook entitled *Money and Financial Institutions*. He has published prolifically in the academic and professional literature on asset/liability management, insurance, fixed-income investments, and foreign exchange risk management. Mr. Babbel received his graduate training in finance at the University of Florida. His postdoctoral education in insurance was undertaken at the Wharton School.

H. Gifford Fong is president of Gifford Fong Associates. He is on the editorial boards of *The Journal of Portfolio Management* and the *Financial Analysts Journal*, and he contributed to *Managing Investment Portfolios: A Dynamic Process*, an ICFA-sponsored text on portfolio management. He serves as program chairman and a member of the board of directors for the Institute for Quantitative Research in Finance. He is also a member of the editorial advisory board for *The Handbook of Fixed Income Securities*. Mr. Fong formerly served as institutional director for the Financial Management Association and as a member of the advisory board for the Investment Technology Association in New York. Mr. Fong is coauthor of *Fixed Income Portfolio Management* and has authored numerous trade journal publications. He attended the University of California, where he earned his B.S., M.B.A., and J.D. degrees.

Jack L. Gibson is a senior consultant in the National Life Actuarial Practice of Coopers & Lybrand. He has worked with numerous large insurance companies in the areas of asset/liability management, actuarial appraisals, and demutualization. Prior to joining Coopers & Lybrand, Mr. Gibson was an associate actuary with Nationwide Life Insurance Company, where he was first involved in extensive product development and then headed the Individual Life Financial Reporting Area. He is a Fellow in the Society of Actuaries and a member of the American Academy of Actuaries. Mr. Gibson received his bachelor's degree in mathematics and statistics from Miami University.

Martin L. Leibowitz is director of the Fixed-Income Research Department at Salomon Brothers, Inc., where he has recently been appointed to the firm's Executive Committee. Mr. Leibowitz serves on the Executive Council of the New York Academy of Sciences and is a member of the board of the Institute for Quantitative Research in Finance. He has written or coauthored more than 100 articles on a wide variety of topics, many of which were published in the *Financial Analysts Journal* and *The Journal of Portfolio Management*. Mr. Leibowitz's recent work includes a series of studies on asset allocation, the shortfall approach to risk management, and the "franchise" effect in security valuation. Five of his papers have received Graham and Dodd Awards for excellence in financial writing from the Financial Analysts Federation. In 1990, Mr. Leibowitz was awarded the Outstanding Financial Executive Award by the Financial Management Association. He received his bachelor's and master's degrees from the University of Chicago and his doctorate in mathematics from New York University.

Robert J. Matczak is a consulting actuary in the National Life Actuarial Services Division of Coopers & Lybrand. His expertise lies in the areas of merger and acquisition appraisal work, asset/liability cash flow analysis, product development, and financial reporting and analysis with emphasis on such interest-sensitive products as universal life, single premium whole life, individual deferred annuities, group annuity, and guaranteed investment contracts. Prior to joining Coopers & Lybrand, Mr. Matczak was a consulting actuary in the Philadelphia Life Practice of Milliman & Robertson. Mr. Matczak also spent several years as chief financial officer at Provident Mutual Life Insurance Company's Group Pension Business Unit. He is a Fellow in the Society of Actuaries and a member of the American Academy of Actuaries. Mr. Matczak received his bachelor's degree in mathematics from Drexel University.

Josie McElhone is director of interest rate risk management at the Federal Home Loan Mortgage Corporation (Freddie Mac), where she has also served as manager of portfolio strategies in the Corporate Finance Department and as senior economist and editor of Freddie Mac's quarterly journal, *Secondary Mortgage Markets*. Previously, Ms. McElhone served as a financial economist at the Federal Home Loan Bank Board, now the Office of Thrift Supervision. She has published numerous articles on financial institution regulation, mortgage instruments, and secondary market issues. She received her B.A. in economics from the University of Texas at Austin and her Ph.D. in economics from Iowa State University.

Thomas E. Messmore, CFA, is senior vice president for the Travelers Insurance Company and is responsible for the Securities Department. He is also chairman of Travelers Asset Management Company, vice chairman of Prospect Company, chairman of Travelers Mortgage Securities Corporation, and a director of Travelers Investment Management Company. Previously, he served as senior vice president and chief financial officer of the Keystone Massachusetts Group in Boston, a Travelers subsidiary. He also served as president of Keystone Real Estate Company and was treasurer of several Keystone mutual funds, the Massachusetts Company, and Travelers Income Properties-I. Mr. Messmore is both a member of AIMR and the Hartford Society of Financial Analysts, Inc. He serves on the Investment Committees of the Metropolitan Hartford YMCA, Hartford Public Library, University of Hartford, and Bushnell Memorial. Mr. Messmore received a B.S. degree in engineering from West Virginia University and an M.B.A. from Harvard Business School.

Phillip D. Parker is an associate general counsel at the Securities and Exchange Commission. As head of the Counseling Section, Mr. Parker is responsible for the legislative and advisory activities of the Office of the General Counsel. In addition to advising the commission on legal and policy issues that arise from enforcement and regulation recommendations, the Counseling Section drafts legislation, develops the commission's position on pending bills in Congress, and prepares testimony for congressional hearings. Prior to his work with the General Counsel, Mr. Parker was a member of the commission's Division of Enforcement, where he served as the division's chief counsel for two years. He is a recipient of the Philip A. Loomis, Jr., Award and the Chairman's Award for Excellence. He is an adjunct professor at the Georgetown University Law Center and frequently serves on the faculty of continuing legal education programs concerning the federal securities laws. Mr. Parker received his A.B. degree summa cum laude from Kenyon College and a J.D. from the University of Virginia.

Alfred Weinberger is a director in the Bond Portfolio Analysis Group of Salomon Brothers, Inc., where he manages the Insurance Asset/Liability Unit. His responsibilities include the development of quantitative approaches and tools to assist insurers in asset allocation and asset/liability management decisions. He has extensive experience in the areas of immunization and dedicated portfolios and was an originator with Martin L. Leibowitz of the fixed-income portfolio management technique known as Contingent Immunization. He joined the firm as a senior analyst in 1980, was promoted to vice president in 1981, and assumed his current position in January 1988. Prior to joining Salomon Brothers, Mr. Weinberger was an assistant treasurer in the Investment Department of the Sun Life Assurance Company of Canada. Mr. Weinberger has had papers published in *The Journal of Portfolio Management* and the *Financial Analysts Journal*. He holds master's degrees in electrical engineering and business.

Eliot P. Williams, CFA, heads the Portfolio Management Division of the Securities Department at the Travelers Insurance Company. He also serves as president and chief operating officer of Travelers Asset Management International, which manages domestic fixed-income portfolios for outside clients of the company. Previously, Mr. Williams held positions in Travelers Investment Management Company, a Travelers subsidiary, as analyst, director of research, and eventually president and chief investment officer. Mr. Williams is a member of both the ICFA Board of Trustees and the AIMR Board of Governors, is on the editorial board of the *CFA Digest*, and is a member of the Investment Research Committee of the American Council of Life Insurance. He is also a former president of the Hartford Society of Financial Analysts, Inc. Mr. Williams received his B.A. in economics from Haverford College and his M.B.A. from the University of Virginia. He also attended the Executive Program at the University of California at Berkeley.

Managing Asset/Liability Portfolios— An Overview

Eliot P. Williams, CFA
Vice President
The Travelers Insurance Company

New ideas have developed during the past few years in the understanding and practice of asset/liability management. Although many of these ideas surfaced in response to the challenges and difficulties many financial institutions faced in the 1980s, they also extend the underlying precepts of modern portfolio theory into new areas of application and make use of some new tools for risk management.

In many ways, the term "asset/liability management" is now obsolete. Increasingly, the objective function is recognized to be surplus optimization within multiple constraints. Surplus duration and the economic value of surplus have now become focal points. The Securities and Exchange Commission and other regulators have begun to call for banks, thrifts, and insurance companies to mark their assets *and liabilities* to market as a fundamental basis for evaluating financial condition.

As a result of this thinking, greater attention is being directed toward defining and monitoring the risks associated with surplus. Here, some of the underlying premises of modern portfolio theory have had to be recast. The risk-free asset is not one without volatility but rather one that best funds the expected cash flow stream of the liabilities. Also, diversification is not in and of itself desirable if the liabilities are highly interest rate sensitive. Further, because liabilities increasingly possess embedded options, analysis that depends on assumptions of normal distributions may be seriously flawed.

Out of these new understandings have grown new tools and techniques for managing the relationship of assets and liabilities—that is, surplus. Options, futures, and swaps are now commonly used to modify cash flow patterns and interest rate sensitivities. Greater attention is given to call characteristics of bonds and of structured securities. Active management techniques are increasingly being applied to liabilities, as well as assets, through acquisition, disposition, and transformation strategies. New approaches to asset allocation incorporate liabilities as a negative asset class and take into account constraints, business flows, and factor sensitivities in developing optimal asset mix combinations. New

performance measurement practices are based on benchmark portfolios of publicly available securities that emulate the relevant liability characteristics.

Managing Under Shortfall Constraints

Leibowitz opened the seminar with the first of several presentations that offer a quantitative framework for constructing portfolios that optimize economic surplus—the difference between the current value of assets and the present value of liabilities. Leibowitz's specific focus is on a methodology that seeks to maximize asset returns within defined loss constraints for both asset values and surplus. After reviewing the mechanics of a traditional asset allocation model to develop an efficient return/variance frontier, Leibowitz introduces liabilities, particularly those with interest rate sensitivity, into the model. The inclusion of liability considerations changes the focus of optimization from asset returns to returns on surplus. In a surplus-optimization framework, asset risks take on new meaning. The risk-free asset is an immunized portfolio that has the same duration as the liabilities. Long bonds become less risky to the extent that they match liability duration; cash becomes more risky because of its failure to match liability duration; and although equities bear greater risk, they also diversify the overall portfolio because they are relatively uncorrelated with bonds and liabilities.

Leibowitz then establishes risk limitations, or shortfall constraints, on both asset loss and surplus loss. He uses the example of a pension plan with a normal mix of 60 percent stocks and 40 percent bonds. First, given assumptions about expected returns, standard deviations, and correlation coefficients for stocks, bonds, and cash, he determines the set of asset portfolios that ensure a 90 percent probability of exceeding the shortfall return. Next, given assumptions about liability durations, he defines a distribution of possible portfolios that meet probabilistic requirements for minimum levels of return on surplus. The possibilities include portfolios with both short- and long-duration mismatch and equity holdings, creating what is sure to become known as the "Leibowitz Egg," an oval-shaped array of asset portfolios that fulfill the surplus shortfall condition. The overlap of the asset shortfall constraint and the surplus shortfall portfolios establishes the universe of possible asset combinations. This model also provides insights into the impact of equities on asset/liability risk management and on the trade-offs of interest rate risk and equity risk in maximizing surplus return.

Modeling Risk Factors

In a highly technical discussion, Fong describes an asset/liability management process in terms of continuous-time mathematics. Fong notes that assets and liabilities can be represented as a collection of cash flows that are affected by different risk factors, which will influence their respective market values. Among the critical risk factors are interest rates, market volatility, and exchange rates (if the portfolio includes foreign securities). Credit, equity, and other forms of risk that may also be important could be addressed separately in this model.

A continuous-time characterization of the term structure has the desirable feature of using diffusion processes instead of specific scenarios of interest rate forecasts. This technique tends to be more computationally efficient than Monte Carlo simulation, which typically contains one stochastic factor—the short rate—and a constant-volatility assumption. Fong makes the important point that volatility is not constant and should be considered a stochastic factor. Therefore, models that assume fixed volatility are flawed in their determination of a representative equilibrium pricing equation, and managers should recognize changing volatility as a source of risk and return. Incorporating both duration and volatility exposure into the volatility term structure model provides a more complete explanation of price change.

The efficient frontier in Fong's model is a set of optimal portfolios derived by using expected rates of return for assets and liabilities and the full-covariance matrix between all pairs of assets and liabilities. The minimum-risk portfolio on this frontier will match total duration of assets with liabilities, and it will match partial durations at each factor rate to account for any potential shifts in different segments of the yield curve. Further, it will match volatility exposure and exchange rate exposure, if present. This minimum-risk portfolio, with its associated expected return and risk characteristics, becomes the benchmark portfolio for the liabilities. To improve upon this return, a manager must move out on the

efficient return and accept additional risk.

Asset Allocation Techniques

Weinberger introduces concepts of business strategy and economic sensitivities into the analysis. Using a property/casualty insurance company as a model, Weinberger provides a quantitative framework for developing an optimum asset allocation strategy with considerations of asset-risk returns, asset/liability relationships, and business strategy. The traditional Markowitz efficient frontier for assets is expanded to treat liabilities as a negative asset class and to focus on the return and risk pattern of surplus as the objective function. Whereas pension funds have become more sensitized to this issue with the implementation of Financial Accounting Standard No. 87, the analysis for insurance companies is complicated by differences among book, generally accepted accounting principles (GAAP), and statutory accounting principles.

Weinberger proposes an analytical framework that recognizes an institution as a dynamic, ongoing concern. As such, it must consider not just its current asset and liability mix but also its operating cash flows and business strategies. Weinberger recognizes that assets and liabilities may be correlated through other factor influences, so his model incorporates a covariance matrix that considers the macroeconomic factors of interest rates, inflation, and real Gross National Product and the microeconomic influences of liability characteristics, insurance pricing patterns, and specific asset risks.

His model also takes into account that the real-world environment may impose constraints—minimum surplus requirements, tax considerations, liquidity needs, or other issues related to actuarial certification. The model also deals with expected leverage of the balance sheet and encompasses a probabilistic analysis of elements in the horizon balance sheet that may affect asset optimization at the beginning of the period. The combination of these features provides an important, insightful framework for considering and addressing critical issues of business strategy and investment strategy.

Liabilities: The Important Investment Issues

Presentations by Gibson and Matczak provide important insights into the characteristics of insurance company liabilities and ways to manage them. Gibson reviews the various types of liabilities of life insurance, property/casualty insurance, and non-insurance financial companies. He notes that the liabilities of the four basic types of life insurance (traditional life, interest-sensitive life, variable life, and annuities) have different types and magnitudes of risk. With traditional life, risk is low because the company's actual experience is retrospectively paid back to policyholders in the form of dividends. In contrast, interest-sensitive life liabilities require an immediate payback of the actual experience through adjustment of insurance premiums or credited rates. Some liability contracts, such as universal life, give policyholders the ability to antiselect if the company's credited interest rate is below that in the external market. Variable life policies transfer particular investment risk to the policyholders. Annuity contracts have liabilities more directly linked to assets and are easier to model than other forms of liability. Property/casualty and noninsurance company liabilities tend to be shorter in nature and therefore less interest rate sensitive.

Gibson notes that insurance liability risks are affected by a variety of external factors, including changes in interest rates and the economic cycle, and such company-specific factors as the distribution system, competition, and sales volume. He briefly reviews how each of these influences might affect the pattern of the liability cash flow and how it should be considered in asset/liability modeling. Like other speakers, Gibson notes the importance of considering both the duration and the convexity of assets and liabilities in analysis. He observes that most life insurance liabilities have durations that are longer than asset durations. Further, in contrast to assets, the liability convexity pattern tends to be concave because of policy lapse rates and policy loan considerations.

Gibson then discusses alternative strategies for managing life insurance liabilities. An interest crediting strategy might include either fixing the interest spread or following the market. Another approach is to offer some form of persistency bonus to agents or policyholders. Dividend and pricing policies can also influence the characteristics of new liabilities.

Matczak discusses several uses for asset/liability modeling, including analyses of risk, interest rate crediting strategies, and investment strategies; merger and acquisition work; and strategic planning. For risk analysis, typically performed by a valuation actuary, the goal is to meet reserve-adequacy requirements as determined by state insurance departments. Increasingly, risk analysis is also being conducted to determine target or required surplus levels and to estimate a company's liability in the face of alternative interest rate or economic scenarios.

Modeling interest rate crediting and investment strategies is becoming an important application of asset/liability management. Further, developing business strategy and determining the sensitivity of that strategy to critical assumptions about such factors as premium payments, mortality experience, and expenses require analysis of both assets and liabilities to determine which strategies are more viable.

Matczak notes that, historically, analysis for mergers and acquisitions and for strategic planning has focused on liabilities alone. The recent experience of a number of companies with asset problems is resulting in more detailed analysis of assets on the balance sheet and closer modeling of the asset cash flows and liquidity positions with the liabilities. He suggests that modeling is becoming increasingly complex and important, particularly in the face of outside influences such as regulation, changing standards of practice, and increased scrutiny by ratings agencies and auditors.

Managing Surplus

Messmore begins by pointing out that banks, thrifts, and insurance companies are all financial intermediaries and have many common characteristics. Managing surplus is a generic concept, applicable and relevant to all financial intermediaries.

Reviewing the evolution of asset/liability management, Messmore notes that accounting rules are focused on a liability-driven business. As a result, recent financial service industry surprises have tended to occur on the asset side because mismatch risk, credit risk, and liquidity risk were not understood by the existing regulatory bodies. This is changing.

To achieve true asset/liability management will require greater understanding by managements, regulators, and investors of asset/liability management concepts; realization that assets and liabilities are fungible concepts; and accounting standards that allow consistent treatment of assets and liabilities and fair comparisons of risks.

The present definition of surplus as the difference between the historic cost of assets less the estimated future value of liabilities is essentially meaningless. As financial services companies broaden their focus to include assets as well as liabilities, the accounting system must change. Appropriate asset/liability management and investment decisions can only be made in a market value world in which the true worth of assets is known.

As a better basis for determining the market value of assets and liabilities, Messmore introduces the concept of an Obligatory Asset Liability swap. Companies would be allowed to short or purchase options on up to 10 percent of the assets or liabilities on other companies' books at their year-end reported values less a 10 percent bid–ask spread. The concept is that the market would force companies to mark assets and liabilities reasonably or run the risk of having either assets or liabilities called away from them.

Messmore then reviews the concept of "duration of surplus" and offers useful insights into the interest rate sensitivity of surplus as well as into tools to help manage surplus. Using the example of a property/casualty company, he shows that any mismatch between assets and liabilities has a magnified effect on surplus because of financial leverage, that financial leverage can be used to increase or decrease the interest rate sensitivity of a firm's economic wealth, and that the influence of duration of surplus dominates earnings per share as an explanatory variable of movements in the stock price of property/casualty companies.

Messmore concludes with the observation that asset/liability management is a classic optimization problem. The goal is to maximize utility based on expected returns, risks, transaction costs, various constraints, and the cost of failing to achieve various target levels or constraints. Although the exercise is relatively straightforward and can be solved with quadratic equations, the task of defining a company's utility, the constraints, and the covariance between the constraints is quite difficult.

Market Value Accounting

Parker reviews the historical position of the SEC on accounting issues, noting that for 40 years, it regarded historic cost accounting as "factual." Then, high rates of inflation in the 1970s led to growing recognition of the failure of historic cost accounting to reflect economic reality. In the 1980s, the thrift crisis gave further notice of the need to modify accounting standards, as institutions that were economically insolvent continued to operate under the protection of the Federal Deposit Insurance Corporation. Parker doubts that the use of market value accounting would have prevented the thrift crisis, but he argues it might have contained the damage by exposing the true significance of political and regulatory policy decisions made during the 1980s.

A more comprehensive approach to market value accounting is now under consideration. It would require reports by financial institutions to reflect the fair market value of their assets, liabilities, and off-balance-sheet items. This would enable regulators and investors to assess more precisely the true economic value and risk exposure of a depository institution. It would also make the managers of

financial institutions more accountable for their investment and business decisions and eliminate the incentive to base business decisions on accounting rather than economic considerations (the most notorious form of this behavior being "gains trading").

Opponents of market value accounting argue that it depends too heavily on subjective appraisals and estimates, that it would necessarily undermine the reality as well as the comparability of financial statements, and that it would increase the potential for fraud in financial statements. In Parker's mind, however, the question is not whether market value accounting can be as precise as historical cost accounting, but whether responsible estimates of market value would be more useful and credible than precise measures of historic costs.

Separate issues relating to market value accounting involve the distinction financial institutions make between their "trading" and their "investment" portfolios. Parker notes that the economic environment that led to the use of asset/liability management strategy undermines the presumption that investment securities will be held to maturity; in practice, management's intent to hold securities has proven virtually impossible for auditors and others to validate. The Financial Accounting Standards Board (FASB) is expected within the next few months to issue an exposure draft concerning the measurement of investment securities. Apparently, FASB will include certain "related liabilities" on a marked-to-market basis in tandem with investment securities.

Measuring Investment Performance

Babbel picks up on the earlier discussions of the importance of asset/liability management and market value accounting by offering a framework for evaluating investment performance. He notes that performance measurement among insurance companies has traditionally had an accounting focus rather than a firm-value focus—that is, a focus on maximizing the value of owners' equity. Because accounting statements are based on book values rather than market values, companies have traditionally relied on yield as the primary performance measurement criterion. This approach is flawed, because high yields may simply reflect underlying credit, liquidity, call, currency, or duration mismatch risks. In fact, modern valuation technologies for mortgages, corporate bonds, and insurance liabilities recognize that yield and return are not the same thing. Fair market values and total return should be used in evaluating investment performance because they account for all the risks in the portfolio.

Within the finance domain, Babbel observes that managers can act to increase firm value in four ways. First, they can invest in projects or financial securities with positive net present values. Second, they can alter the company's financial structure and assume more or less leverage as is considered appropriate. Third, they can adjust the company's duration and convexity mismatches. Babbel notes that although studies have shown that better-matched companies command higher stock prices relative to their economic surplus, some companies may have reasons for deliberately mismatching durations. Fourth, they can try to earn more on the firm's assets than it pays on its liabilities, perhaps by issuing liabilities on favorable terms through cost-efficient distribution networks or by exercising superior timing, valuation, or liquidity-management skills.

The performance measurement system Babbel proposes is designed to measure the performance of assets relative to liabilities on the basis of fair market values and total rates of return. The first step is to characterize each of the liabilities by its market characteristics (duration, convexity, volatility, etc.) to establish liability benchmark portfolios. These benchmark portfolios contain actively traded securities that behave over time in a manner that closely parallels that of the actual liabilities. Benchmarks may be established for separate sets of liability groupings and then aggregated into an overall liability benchmark. Next, the firm should establish an asset proxy portfolio, which may differ from the liability benchmark portfolio to the extent that investment policy determines that more credit risk, call risk, or interest rate risk than exists in the liability portfolio is appropriate. The asset proxy portfolio may consist of several sub-asset proxy portfolios representing individual asset classes such as corporates, mortgages, municipals, and high-yield equities. Last, the benchmarks must be adjusted to account for any constraints (liquidity, duration, convexity, credit quality, and minimum-yield requirements) that limit active management decisions.

The performance measurement process consists of comparing actual results against these established benchmarks. The actual liability experience should be compared with the results of the liability benchmark portfolio. Investment policy is evaluated by comparing the asset proxy portfolio with the liability benchmark portfolios. Finally, the results of individual asset class managers should be reviewed against the sub-asset proxy portfolios.

Babbel concludes by noting that in the long run, the time, effort, and expense required to measure total return—and to reward performance that enhances total return—should be justified by an increase in the value of the firm.

Asset/Liability Management Case Study

McElhone provides a refreshing and interesting description of the current practice of asset/liability management at the Federal Home Loan Mortgage Corporation (Freddie Mac). Freddie Mac is acutely sensitive to asset/liability management and, reinforcing the statements of a number of speakers, holds that market value surplus is far superior to book capital or GAAP capital as a measure of the current economic capital of the firm. Freddie Mac has produced market value balance sheets since 1989.

Much of McElhone's discussion focuses on the processes and procedures Freddie Mac uses in arriving at its market values and measuring interest rate risk. She notes the distinctive feature of guarantee fees, which are the fees earned for insuring the book of business. These fees are typically 25 basis points of the unpaid principal balance of loans, and they represent nearly 60 percent of Freddie Mac's total market net worth.

Freddie Mac uses three methods to value assets: market quotes for long-term debt and debentures; book values for assets and liabilities with maturities of 60 days or fewer; and financial modeling, particularly option-based models, for mortgages and guarantee fees. She notes that Freddie Mac's market value has been remarkably stable over time, despite a 150-basis-point decline in interest rates.

McElhone also discusses the importance of understanding and matching both the duration and the convexity of assets and liabilities. The interest rate sensitivity of the guarantee fees is somewhat problematic because market values are influenced by mortgage prepayments and replacements. Analysis suggests that the two influences largely offset each other so that a relatively flat curve exists for the interest rate sensitivity of the guarantee fees.

McElhone concludes by discussing some of the analytical problems Freddie Mac faces in its work. Because there is no effective basis for determining what level of risk is appropriate for the firm, they have not defined a shortfall constraint. McElhone also notes the limitations of the assumption that yield curves shift instantaneously and permanently. Despite these limitations, market value accounting is used in Freddie Mac's incentive plans, in its reports to the board of directors and senior management, and in discussions with equity analysts. The company maintains that awareness of market value accounting is growing and that eventually it will be applied to the full accounting system.

Setting the Stage

Martin L. Leibowitz
Director, Fixed-Income Research Department
Salomon Brothers, Inc.

Liabilities have more subtleties, contingencies, complexities, and noise than sometimes thought. Because many liabilities pose complex concerns, trying to get a strict optimization is difficult. Optimization models tend to focus on simplistic problems that can be solved. A "balancing" model provides a more realistic description of practical asset/liability problems.

The asset/liability problem is more general than the asset-only problem, although different financial intermediaries face different types of asset/liability problems. The asset-only case is a variation of the asset/liability problem in which the liability is cash. This presentation provides an asset allocation methodology for constructing portfolios that strike a balance between asset performance and maintenance of acceptable levels of downside risk in both asset and surplus contexts.[1]

The Asset/Liability Framework

The importance of surplus measurement differs for each type of financial intermediary. **Figure 1** indicates for different types of investment situations how the importance of surplus management changes as you alter the horizon over which surplus performance must be assessed. The importance of the surplus measure can range from being all-encompassing (as in spread banking) to almost insignificant for some highly funded corporate and public pension funds. For pension funds that have strong sponsoring entities, liabilities may play a small role because the sponsoring organization is there to pay the bills and the liabilities are fuzzy and distant in time. In these cases, maximizing the asset returns for a given level of risk makes more sense than worrying about the surplus measure.

The Asset-Only Framework

The asset-only framework is a good place to begin, because it is familiar to everyone. **Figure 2** shows the traditional presentation of the risk/reward trade-offs among stocks, bonds, and cash. Many investors make asset allocation decisions using this approach. The traditional framework offends fixed-income analysts because bonds are shown as a single point, whereas in fact a continuum of fixed-income instruments is available. **Figure 3** shows the efficient frontier in an asset-only framework using the entire yield curve. From this perspective, the original efficient portfolio is probably inefficient. Moreover, in a liability environment in which the liabilities almost inevitably have certain interest rate sensitivity, consideration of the yield curve continuum is critical.

The Surplus Framework

Surplus is defined as the difference between the current value of the assets and the present value of the liabilities. Risk changes when one moves from the asset-only framework to the surplus framework. Using the simplest of liabilities in the pension fund environment—the accumulated benefit obligation (ABO)—**Figure 4** shows how the riskiness of equities, bonds, and cash changes from the asset-only framework to the surplus framework. Everything shifts and changes. Long bonds suddenly become less risky. One of those long bonds will become the riskless asset, as cash was in the asset-only framework. Cash itself becomes fairly risky because of the uncertainty in reinvestment rates during the period over which the liabilities are discharged. Equities, because their returns are relatively uncorrelated with those of the liability, become slightly more risky. **Figure 5** shows the risk/return trade-off for eq-

---

[1]This presentation is based on M.L. Leibowitz, S. Kogelman, and L.N. Bader, "Asset Performance and Surplus Control: A Dual-Shortfall Approach," Salomon Brothers, Inc. (July 1991).

Figure 1. The Importance of Asset/Liability Management

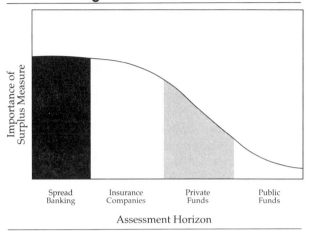

Source: Salomon Brothers, Inc.

Figure 2. Asset-Only Framework

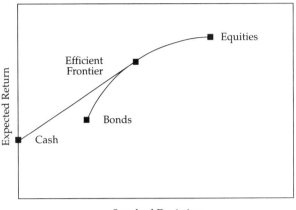

Source: Salomon Brothers, Inc.

uities compared to a continuum of fixed-income instruments in an ABO surplus framework. The fixed-income instruments form a broken curve. The instruments with durations longer than the liability are still risky, but as the durations shrink down to that of the liability, the risk lessens. The immunizing portfolio, which has the same duration as the liability, becomes the riskless asset. Cash and the shorter duration instruments become risky in this surplus context. The yield curve in a surplus framework looks almost like a reflection of the yield curve in the asset-only framework. Equities are still risky, but their prospective returns are alluring.

The Asset Portfolio

The shortfall technique can be used to balance asset risk and surplus risk with respect to an ABO. Returning to the asset-only framework, **Figure 6** shows the risk/return trade-off for stock/bond portfolios using

a 60/40 allocation as a benchmark asset portfolio. Stocks are assumed to have an expected return of 13 percent and a standard deviation of 17 percent. Bonds, represented by the Salomon Brothers Broad Investment-Grade Bond (BIG) Index with a duration of 4.64 years, are expected to return 8 percent with a standard deviation of 7 percent. The stock/bond correlation is 0.35. Based on these assumptions, the benchmark portfolio has an expected return of 11 percent and a standard deviation of 11.5 percent.

Figure 7 shows the efficient stock/bond frontier for varying bond durations, assuming that all bonds are yielding 8 percent. As the duration of the bond increases, the efficient frontier becomes increasingly bow-shaped. At the other extreme, where duration is zero (cash), the efficient frontier is a straight line.

The return distribution of the benchmark portfolio is used to calculate the shortfall constraint. **Figure 8** shows the return distribution of the benchmark portfolio. The left-hand tail represents downside

Figure 3. Asset-Only Framework—Using the Entire Yield Curve

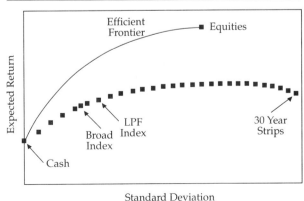

Source: Salomon Brothers, Inc.

Figure 4. Risk Changes in ABO Surplus Framework

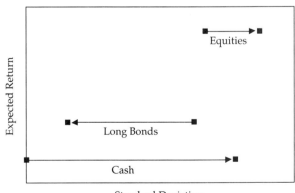

Source: Salomon Brothers, Inc.

Figure 5. ABO Surplus Framework—Using the Entire Yield Curve

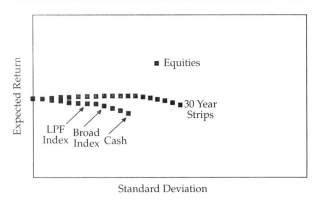

Source: Salomon Brothers, Inc.

Figure 6. The Risk/Return Trade-Off for Stock/Bond Portfolios (Duration = 4.64 Years)

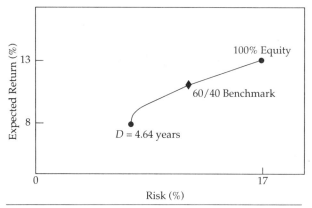

Source: Salomon Brothers, Inc.

risk. One standard deviation below the expected return is a –0.5 percent return. The 10th percentile point—the point at which 10 percent of the probability is to the left—is equal to the mean return, 11 percent, minus 1.28 times the standard deviation, 11.5 percent. In this case, the 10th percentile point is –3.7 percent. In other words, in any single period, there is a 10 percent probability that the return on the portfolio will fall below –3.7 percent and a 90 percent probability that the return will exceed that threshold.

The implicit shortfall constraint is illustrated for the 10th percentile point in **Figure 9**. The –3.7 percent shortfall line passes through the threshold point of –3.7 percent and through the benchmark portfolio point. All points along the shortfall line represent portfolios for which the expected return offsets the portfolio volatility sufficiently to ensure a 90 percent probability that the one-year return will exceed –3.7 percent. Portfolios above the shortfall line have a higher expected return for a given shortfall risk than

portfolios on the line. Consequently, all portfolios above the line have a greater than 90 percent probability that the one-year return will exceed –3.7 percent. The new frontier cuts the asset-only space into two realms: one for which the chance of beating this implicit threshold return is more than 90 percent, and another for which the chance of beating the threshold return is less than 90 percent.

If you do not want the portfolio to fall below the 60/40 portfolio and its implicit shortfall, then you will have to confine the portfolio to the space above the shortfall line, with mixtures of bonds and cash that fall into this region. Because the cash/equity line is the asset-only efficient frontier and because the object is to maximize return, the "optimal" portfolio is found at the point on the cash/equity line that intersects with the shortfall line. This portfolio has a slightly higher equity mixture than the benchmark portfolio and has more cash than bonds.

Figure 7. Efficient Stock/Bond Frontier for Varying Bond Durations

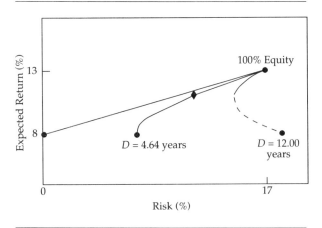

Source: Salomon Brothers, Inc.

Figure 8. The Return Distribution for the Benchmark Portfolio

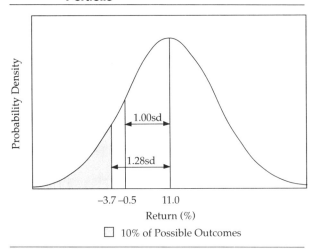

Source: Salomon Brothers, Inc.

Figure 9. The Implicit Shortfall Constraint for the Benchmark Portfolio

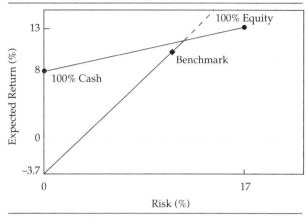

Source: Salomon Brothers, Inc.

The Surplus Return

Surplus return is defined in this case as the change in surplus divided by the initial value of the ABO liability. Different criteria—for example, a focus on funding ratio rather than dollars of surplus—lead to different immunizing portfolios and different asset allocation consequences.

The importance of surplus return can be shown using a 10-year duration ABO liability and a funding ratio that varies between 100 percent and 140 percent. **Table 1** compares the liability and asset returns with the surplus returns in three cases. At a 100 percent funding ratio, the assets match the liabilities dollar for dollar. With liabilities equal to $100 million and an 8 percent expected liability return, liabilities will equal $108 million at the end of the period, without any interim payouts or changes in interest rates. The risk-free asset allocation on a surplus basis would be a 10-year duration immunizing portfolio. If the assets are instead invested in a 60/40 stock/bond portfolio, they have an expected return of 11 percent; that is, expected growth to $111 million. The surplus is expected to grow from zero at the beginning to $3 million at the end.

A 140 percent funding ratio indicates $140 of assets for every $100 of liabilities. To maintain equal dollar duration, the duration of the immunizing portfolio is determined by dividing 10 years by 1.4 or 7.1 years. (For example, a 1 percent increase in interest rates would add 10 percent, or $10 million, to the $100 million liability, and 7.1 percent, or $10 million, to the $140 million asset.) In this case, the expected surplus return is 7.4 percent.

Table 2 summarizes the asset-only and surplus performance of the 60/40 benchmark portfolio, given a 140 percent funding ratio. Although the asset-only performance meets our –3.7 percent minimum return criteria, the surplus performance does not. The benchmark portfolio's expected surplus return is 7.4 percent, and the standard deviation of the surplus return is 14.7 percent. The 10th percentile surplus return is –11.5 percent, so there is a 10 percent chance that surplus will decrease by $11.5 million (11.5 percent of the $100 million initial liability), markedly worse than the –7 percent minimum target.

The Shortfall Curve for the Surplus Return

Pension fund sponsors who wish to achieve stability in the plan's surplus can do so with a bond portfolio that matches the liability in present value, duration, and other volatility characteristics. Such an immunized portfolio will preserve the surplus within some reasonable range of interest rate changes. Most sponsors, however, do not require this degree of safety. Typically, a sponsor with a 140 percent funding ratio might be willing to sustain some surplus risk, provided that the portfolio has substantial upside potential. Usually a sponsor can comfortably tolerate some surplus loss.

Figure 10 illustrates the surplus shortfall curve for a pension fund with a 140 percent funding ratio and a 10-year liability duration. The surplus constraint pattern is far more complicated than the straight line for the asset-only portfolio, and it is represented by an egg-shaped convex curve. Each

Table 1. Liability-Based Surplus Return Example

Funding Ratio (% of liabilities)	Category	Initial Value ($millions)	Final Value ($millions)	Liability or Asset Return	Surplus Return
—	Liability	$100.0	$108.0	8.0%	—
140%	Assets	140.0	155.4	11.0	
	Surplus	40.0	47.4		7.4%
100	Assets	100.0	111.0	11.0	
	Surplus	0.0	3.0		3.0

Source: Salomon Brothers, Inc.

Table 2. Performance Summary for the Benchmark Portfolio (60% Stock/40% BIG Index; Funding Ratio = 140%)

Measure	Current Expected Return	Current Standard Deviation	Current 10th Percentile Return	Target 10th Percentile Return
Asset-only performance	11.0%	11.5%	–3.7%	–3.7%
Surplus performance	7.4	14.7	–11.5	–7.0

Source: Salomon Brothers, Inc.

point within the egg represents an asset portfolio that fulfills the surplus shortfall condition. The benchmark portfolio and the immunizing portfolio points are included for reference. The immunizing portfolio is an all-bond portfolio that has the same dollar sensitivity to interest rate changes as the liability. The duration of the immunizing portfolio is 7.1 years—that is, the 10-year duration divided by the 140 percent funding ratio.

Let me try to provide an intuitive understanding of the shortfall curve. First, note that the leftmost point on the curve represents a 100 percent bond portfolio with a 3.4-year duration. This is the shortest duration all-bond portfolio for which the probability is at most 10 percent that the surplus return will be –7 percent or less. For any all-bond portfolios with shorter duration, the gap between the bond duration and the immunizing portfolio is too large, and the tenth-percentile surplus return will fall below –7 percent.

To the right are all-bond portfolios with durations that are closer to the 7.1-year immunizing duration. Consequently, such portfolios will have better shortfall performance than the 3.4-year duration

Figure 10. The Surplus Shortfall Curve (–7% Surplus Threshold)

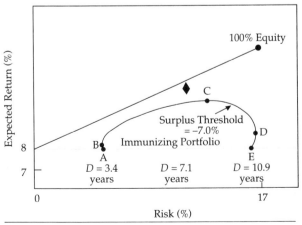

Source: Salomon Brothers, Inc.

portfolio. To the far right of the curve is a portfolio with a 10.9-year duration. Note that the 3.4-year duration and the 10.9-year duration are equidistant from the 7.1-year duration immunizing portfolio. Both of these portfolios have the same duration gap and therefore the same –7 percent surplus shortfall threshold. The duration gap, combined with the volatility of interest rates, which is assumed to be 150 basis points, will produce exactly the surplus return volatility allowed by the shortfall constraint.

As equity is added to the portfolio, the expected return will increase, because equity provides a 5 percent expected return premium over the fixed-income return. In addition, the low correlation between equity and the liability at first causes the surplus volatility to increase more slowly than the surplus return. Consequently, the initial additions of equity actually improve the surplus shortfall level, and the shortfall curve bubbles slightly to the left as we move upward from the 3.4-year duration point. A point is reached, however, where further equity additions cause the surplus volatility to increase very rapidly. To compensate for this equity-related volatility, the bond duration must be increased so as to bring the asset portfolio duration closer to the immunizing duration and eliminate interest-rate risk. With more equities, the equity risk becomes dominant and the curve flattens.

Despite the arguments in favor of surplus management, few portfolio managers or plan sponsors have adopted it. When FAS No. 87 was adopted, everyone was worried that the pension world was going to shift totally to a surplus-only world—that is, immunize portfolios, eliminate any kind of risks, and do it against ABOs. That did not happen for several reasons, not the least of which is that the funding ratios were so assuringly high when FAS No. 87 was implemented. Another reason is that sponsors were reluctant to put too much faith in a very narrowly defined and very accounting-driven definition of liabilities. They recognized that the full plan liabilities go far beyond the ABO, that they are multiperiod liabilities rather than single-period liabilities, and that the valuation system contained a lot of tolerance for accepting adverse movements in the ABO surplus—as long as everything else remained intact.

In this situation, few corporations made major changes in their asset allocations. To many portfolio managers and sponsors, moving out of a long-term stance in equities—believed to be the long-term asset of choice—totally into fixed-income securities that had a volatility of their own was very distasteful and discomforting. One can argue whether that was right or wrong, but it was a fact.

Given that fact and given the rationale behind it, the issue becomes how to address liability issues while still paying attention to the asset problem.

Asset Performance and Surplus Control

The situation can be resolved by putting the two shortfall conditions together. Dealing with asset-only space is an advantage because people are comfortable with it. Dealing with surplus space is important because it recognizes the impact of liabilities. **Figure 11** puts these two shortfall conditions together. The benchmark portfolio lies outside the surplus shortfall curve corresponding to a minimum surplus return of –7 percent, as we saw in Table 2. The point of intersection between the asset-only line and the surplus egg corresponds to the portfolio with the highest expected return that meets both the shortfall requirements. This dual shortfall portfolio consists of 44 percent stocks and 56 percent bonds with a 6.6-year duration.

Thus far, we have arbitrarily imposed a –7 percent threshold on the surplus return and have assumed that the –3.7 percent asset-only threshold

should be maintained. More often, however, the problem is determining the appropriate balance between asset-only and surplus risks. The entire risk/return diagram can be covered by a grid of shortfall lines and shortfall curves, as **Figure 12** shows. Within the grid, the portfolio manager must select an appropriate surplus shortfall curve and a suitable asset shortfall line. The highest intersection point of the selected line and curve represents a balanced portfolio that meets the dual-shortfall condition. As the surplus constraint is tightened, the desired portfolio moves closer to the immunizing portfolio. As the asset constraint is tightened, the desired portfolio moves closer to cash. Not surprisingly, these constraints pull in different directions. When no intersection point exists, either the asset or the surplus shortfall requirement (or both) must be relaxed before a suitable portfolio can be found.

Conclusion

This is a paradigm that can be applied broadly. It can be useful not only for gaining intuitions about the problems that face us but also for solving some of them in reasonable, balanced ways. I should emphasize that liabilities deserve a lot more scrutiny and investigation than they typically get. The liabilities that confront us have more subtleties, contingencies, complexities, and noise, and they are less cleanly correlated with interest rates than we allow for in our thinking and our models. Many of these liabilities pose complex concerns, so trying to get a strict optimization is not only difficult, it may be wrong. Optimization models tend to focus attention on a simplistic problem that can be solved, but the framework is dangerously vulnerable to the potential surprises. The "balancing" model better describes the asset/liability problems that arise in practice.

Figure 11. A Portfolio that Meets Both Asset-Only and Surplus Shortfall Constraints

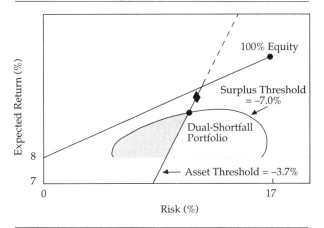

Figure 12. The Shortfall Grid

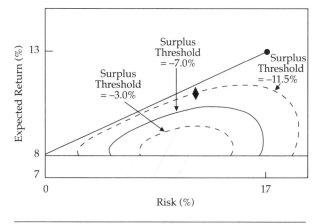

Question and Answer Session

Martin L. Leibowitz

Question: You show the efficient frontier for ABO surplus. How different would that frontier look for a projected benefit obligation (PBO) surplus?

Leibowitz: Actually, I did not show any efficient frontiers for the surplus case. They are there, but they are hidden. They will always be generally egg-shaped. They will orient themselves in different dimensions and have different positions depending on the nature of the correlation with fixed-income, equity, or whatever assets you have. With the kind of random noise embedded in that liability, they will be different but generally egg-shaped with some orientation in this space and around some central point.

Question: What would be the effect on the surplus shortfall curve assuming a positively sloped yield curve and a negative yield curve?

Leibowitz: The real issue is to get an expected return curve. Academics argue that the return curve is either flat or that the slope reflects the liquidity premium required by the holders of longer duration bonds. Clearly, different return curves would change the character of these shortfall patterns, but under a fairly wide range of both positive and negative yields, they would not change that much. It does not totally change the character of the solution.

Question: You use bond duration in your analysis. Do total portfolio duration or surplus duration play roles?

Leibowitz: Yes. The total portfolio duration is embedded in the return correlations in a statistical sense. When you create a portfolio of fixed-income assets, which has a defined duration, and equities that have a correlation with the fixed-income portion, this generates an implied correlation with interest rates for the entire portfolio. The implied correlation generates an empirical duration. For a strict optimum portfolio on the surplus side, the duration of the liabilities should be matched dollar for dollar by the total portfolio duration—the combination of the statistical equity duration and fixed-income duration.

Question: Does the shortfall constraint curve reflect a dollar duration match to the liabilities? If so, how are equities treated with regard to duration?

Leibowitz: The durations are embedded. If you were to go to the maximum return point and find the duration of the fixed-income portion that hits the maximum return point on that egg, you would find that the weighted average of the duration of that fixed-income portfolio and the duration of the equity portion implied by the equity/bond correlation would equal the 10-year duration of the immunizing portfolio.

The total portfolio duration concept drives you toward a surplus optimization. If you go to this optimal point by maximizing an expected return from a surplus-only point of view, you can ask yourself, "I am here, I am getting the maximum possible return, so what am I doing wrong from an asset-only point of view?" The answer is, "I am incurring asset-only risk." In my portfolio, I have a very long-duration bond portfolio to compensate for the fact that I have mostly equities, which have very low duration. A strict surplus optimization would take you to a total portfolio duration that equals the liability duration. To match the volatility of the liability, you would be taking on a great deal of interest rate risk in your bonds, introducing asset volatility that would hurt the asset-only performance.

Question: Please elaborate on the risk-free portfolio. If it is not the immunizing portfolio, what is it, and when would the risk-free portfolio be the immunizing portfolio?

Leibowitz: If the problem is that your liabilities have only interest rate sensitivity as the source of volatility, then the immunizing portfolio would be that fixed-income portfolio whose duration is the liability duration divided by the ratio of assets to liabilities. When a liability is correlated with equities or has more noise—like a PBO, which involves a little uncertainty—you cannot get a risk-free match-off. You can get a minimum-risk match-off, and your shortfall egg will be centered in some sense on that minimum risk portfolio, but it will not be a risk-free portfolio.

Question: Would the egg change if we lengthened the time horizon?

Leibowitz: Going to a multiperiod environment is quite fascinating. In terms of an efficient asset-only frontier, cash has the same risk over multiple periods, and equity risk decreases. So the shortfall line will become more steeply sloped. There will also be a slight degradation in the risk return premium. If we reset the asset shortfall threshold appropriately over multiple years instead of wanting at least –3.7 percent over one year with 90 percent probability—that is, we want –3.7 percent a year over three years with, perhaps, 97 percent probability—the shortfall line does not change. In terms of what happens to the eggs, they generally do not change dramatically if you tighten the shortfall constraint to reflect the risk reduction that the longer time horizon brings.

Question: Does this same analysis apply for insurance companies, banks, and other financial institutions?

Leibowitz: Yes, with some alterations. You could argue that for banks, the surplus measure is more important and in some ways better defined but that the surplus measure is artificially tight. Spread banking has not paid sufficient attention to the fact that surplus is just an accounting measure that does not consider credit quality of the underlying assets. Banks have that problem, and insurance companies have the problem in spades.

Utilizing Concepts of Modern Portfolio Theory in an Asset/Liability Management Context

H. Gifford Fong
President
Gifford Fong Associates

Various factors go into solving for an asset/liability-efficient portfolio, some of which can be modified to suit individual circumstances. The critical parts of the analysis are the principles of characterizing assets and liabilities in terms of risk factors and the ability to evaluate those risk factors from the perspective of a full covariance analysis.

Asset/liability management can be defined as the process of managing the asset portfolio to maintain or improve the liability funding. Many of the relationships and risk measures involved in asset/liability management can be expressed in terms of continuous-time mathematics. This approach allows a more robust description of and a more flexible approach to some analytical solutions. The general framework for asset/liability management that I will describe provides useful principles from a practical day-to-day standpoint. I will also present a new risk measure that we believe is very relevant for asset/liability management.[1]

Characterization of Assets and Liabilities

The goal of portfolio management is to end up with some form of optimal portfolio. To do so in the asset/liability context, we must first define liabilities, assets, and the sources of risk.

Liabilities are hard to define accurately. In general terms, they can be represented as a composition of liability classes such as fixed cash flows of given amounts at given dates, floating rate or indexed payments, and contingent liabilities. In most cases, a liability can be formulated in terms of its expected cash flows.

Assets can be represented on an individual security level or as a collection of asset classes. As with liabilities, assets can be characterized by a series of cash flows. Examples include the typical fixed-in-come instruments; interest rate contingent claims, which include those fixed-income instruments with embedded options such as callable bonds, sinking fund instruments, and mortgage-backed securities; interest rate options; futures; and foreign securities and currency contracts.

Exposure to Risks

The market value of each asset or liability class is affected by changes in risk factors. The quantification and management of risk can be characterized in terms of identified risk factors, three of which can be immediately identified. The first is factor rates, which are defined as the rates of several key maturities that derive yield curve changes. These factor rates represent various points along the term structure. The sensitivity to interest rate change of an asset or liability can be represented relative to the various factor rates that exist. This is a more precise way of decomposing the total sensitivity of an asset or liability to interest rate changes.

The second risk factor is market volatility. Both assets and liabilities are sensitive to changes in volatility. It is important to capture this dimension of the overall risk of the portfolio.

The third risk factor is exchange rates, if the portfolio includes foreign securities. For most fixed-income asset/liability problems, however, the first two factors cover the usual range of risks.

Changes in the value of each asset or liability class are measured by determining the exposures of the class to changes in the risk factors. Exposure to factor rates is measured by partial durations and

[1]Many of the ideas in this presentation are described in H.G. Fong and O.A. Vasicek, "Fixed-Income Volatility Management," *Journal of Portfolio Management* (Spring 1991):41-46.

partial convexities. Each partial duration is the price sensitivity to a change in one factor rate, with the other factors held constant. Thus, the formula for factor rates is:

$$D_i = -\frac{1}{P}\left(\frac{\partial P}{\partial R_i}\right),$$

where

D_i = partial duration,
P = market value of the asset/liability class, and
R_i = a factor rate.

Using this formula, we can quantify the interest rate sensitivity of an asset or liability to interest rate changes. Volatility exposure is the sensitivity of market value to changes in volatility. It takes a form similar to that of duration:

$$F = -\frac{1}{P}\left(\frac{\partial P}{\partial v}\right),$$

where

F = volatility exposure, and
v = volatility.

Exposure to exchange rates is measured by the sensitivity of value to exchange rate changes:

$$G_i = -\frac{1}{P}\left(\frac{\partial P}{\partial q_i}\right),$$

where

G_i = exchange rate exposure, and
q_i = given exchange rate.

Continuous-Time Models

Term structure models provide an explanation of the behavior of interest rates. A continuous-time characterization of the term structure has the desirable features of using diffusion processes instead of specific scenarios of interest change. These models tend to be more computationally efficient as compared to the alternative of Monte Carlo simulation. As an example of a continuous-time equilibrium term structure, consider:

$$dr = b(r,t)dt + \sigma(r,t)dz,$$

where

dr = change in the short rate,
$b(r,t)$ = $a\,(\bar{r} - r)$ = direction of change,
$\sigma(r,t)$ = standard deviation of changes, and
dz = random element.

This model, which is typical of most current term structure models, contains one stochastic factor—the short rate—and an assumption about volatility. The short rate basically determines the future behavior of interest rates. This particular form of the model may incorporate the assumption of a mean-reverting short rate. This would require the model to conform to an additional condition.

Volatility can be characterized in several ways. First, Vasicek assumes that volatility equals the standard deviation of the short rate, $\sigma(r,t) = \sigma$.[2] Cox, Ingersoll, and Ross assume that volatility equals the standard deviation of the short rate times the square root of that rate, $\sigma(r,t) = \sigma\sqrt{r}$.[3] Dothan assumes that volatility equals the standard deviation of the short rate times the short rate, $\sigma(r,t) = \sigma r$.[4] Although the specific description of volatility may vary somewhat among the preceding approaches, they all share a similar assumption—that volatility is a constant term.

As a further example of the typical assumption made for volatility, consider a representative equilibrium pricing equation. Assuming that the short rate, r, follows a random walk with variance σ^2, then a zero-coupon bond maturing at time t is priced as:

$$P(t) = exp\,(\,-rt + 1/6\,\sigma^2 t^3).$$

By inspection, it can be seen that volatility, σ^2, does enter the equation for the price; that is, it does have an effect on pricing. Therefore, the nature of volatility is an important consideration.

The representative term structure models discussed are based on the assumption that volatility is a constant; in reality, volatility changes with time. It is a stochastic factor. Therefore, to capture the entire range of risk associated with a fixed-income portfolio, analysts must recognize volatility as a source of risk and return. They must be concerned about changes in volatility in addition to changes in the level of rates captured by duration. The sensitivity

[2]O.A. Vasicek, "An Equilibrium Characterization of the Term Structure," *Journal of Financial Economics* 5 (1977):177-88.

[3]J.C. Cox, J.E. Ingersoll, Jr., and S.A. Ross, "A Theory of the Term Structure of Interest Rates," *Econometrica* 53 (1985):385-407.

[4]L.U. Dothan, "On the Term Structure of Interest Rates," *Journal of Financial Economics* 6 (1978):59-69.

of the price of an asset to volatility changes is an important component of the overall risk control of the asset/liability portfolio.

Volatility Management

Volatility management is the investment process that acknowledges that the role of volatility is a source of both risk and return and that changes in volatility must be factored into the overall risk control of the portfolio.

Just as duration measures the change in price for a 1 percent change in the level of interest rates, volatility exposure identifies the sensitivity of price to a 1 percent change in volatility. By incorporating both duration and volatility exposure into the volatility term structure model, we end up with a more complete explanation for price change:

$$P(t) = exp[-rD(t) + vF(t) + N(t)],$$

where

P	=	price of a zero-coupon bond,
t	=	time to maturity,
r	=	short rate,
v	=	volatility,
$D(t)$	=	duration,
$F(t)$	=	volatility exposure, and
$N(t)$	=	normalizing function.

In this framework, the price change is made up of three components—the risk-free rate; the price change attributable to a change in the level of rates, basically a shift in the term structure; and a return component resulting from changes in volatility:

$$\frac{\Delta P}{P} = ER.\Delta t - D\Delta r + F\Delta v,$$

where

$\frac{\Delta P}{P}$	=	percentage price change,
ER	=	expected return,
Δt	=	time interval,
Δr	=	rate change,
Δv	=	volatility change,
D	=	duration, and
F	=	volatility exposure.

In the asset/liability context, the implication of this equation is that the change in level of interest rates and change in level of volatility are the important determinants of the change in price of both assets

and liabilities and are important elements in describing the range of asset and liability risk exposures that exist within a portfolio. If you can control for duration and volatility changes, then you are controlling most, if not all, of the risk for typical fixed-income portfolios.

Expected Returns

To derive a set of portfolios on the efficient frontier, the expected return for each asset and liability must be calculated. Expected return, along with variance and covariance, are necessary inputs for the mean-variance optimization procedure.

The equilibrium expected rate of return is a combination of two components, the risk-free rate and the compensation for risk above the riskless level. The first term, the risk-free rate, provides the base-level return for holding a riskless asset or liability. All assets and liabilities have embedded in them a riskless component. The second term provides compensation for accepting an asset or liability that has risk over and above a riskless asset or liability. The compensation for accepting risk above the risk-free level is determined by the market and is called the market price of risk. The equation for the equilibrium expected return is:

$$E = r + \sum_{i=1}^{m} \lambda_i \, C_i \, \sigma_i,$$

where

E	=	equilibrium expected return,
r	=	risk-free rate of return,
λ_i	=	market price of risk,
c_i	=	risk exposures (D_i, F, G_i), and
σ_i	=	variance of the asset.

The change in the value of an asset or liability is the sum of the risk factor changes multiplied by the risk exposures:

$$\frac{dp}{P} = Edt + \sum_{i=1}^{m} c_i \, dx_i.$$

where

x_i	=	risk factors (D_i, V, q_i),
C_i	=	risk exposures (D_i, F, G_i), and
M	=	number of risk factors.

The first component is the equilibrium expected return associated with the risk of the asset or liability. The second component represents changes in the risk factors; it is directly dependent upon forecasts contributed by the portfolio manager.

The total expected rate of return is the equilibrium expected return plus the changes in the risk factors that are forecast by active managers:

$$E\frac{dp}{P} = Edt + \sum_{i=1}^{M} C_i Edx_i .$$

These formulas illustrate the potential value added by active investors. Passive strategies correspond to the case in which the investor does not possess information different from that of the market. In that case, the total expected return on each asset class is equal to the equilibrium expected return. Passive managers choose not to forecast the future and end up with only the equilibrium expected rate of return. With active strategies, an investor's forecast of the risk factor changes differs from those implied by the market pricing. So the difference between active and passive strategies in this context is whether the investor wants to forecast, and this difference—as shown above—is readily quantified.

Variances and Covariances

The variance of each risk factor provides a measure of its respective uncertainty when considered separately. The covariance measures the relative co-movement between risk factors. Both variances and covariances of each risk factor must be considered to determine the overall riskiness of an asset or liability.

The variance of return on a given asset or liability class is calculated as:

$$S^2 = \sum_{i=}^{m} \sum_{j=1}^{m} C_i C_j \sigma_{ij} ,$$

where

S^2 = variance of return on the asset/liability class, and

σ_{ij} = covariance matrix for the risk factors.

The covariance between two asset or liability classes is calculated as:

$$Cov = \sum_{i=1}^{m} \sum_{j=1}^{m} C_i' C_j'' \sigma_{ij} ,$$

where

C_i' = risk exposures of the first asset/liability class, and

C_j'' = risk exposures of the second asset/liability class.

These are standard calculations that relate the underlying risk factors of each asset to another asset and with each liability to another liability. To capture the risk characteristics of the asset and liability portfolios requires quantification of the underlying variance and covariance of the respective risk factors.

The Minimum-Risk Portfolio

The objective of asset/liability management is to hold a portfolio on the efficient frontier, where the efficient frontier is the difference in the market value of the assets and the market value of the liabilities. The set of optimal portfolios that composes the efficient frontier is derived using the expected rates of return for assets and liabilities and the full covariance matrix between all pairs of assets and liabilities. Each portfolio on the efficient frontier has a specific and unique market value in each asset and liability that determines the portfolio's risk and return characteristics.

To maintain the portfolio on the efficient frontier, it needs to be rebalanced continuously. Ideally, rebalancing would occur at each instantaneous time interval, but this is impractical. In place of instantaneous rebalancing, the rebalancing period can be set to the length of the portfolio manager's time horizon. This still permits use of the continuous-time approach, but in a more practical framework. The long-term goal of funding liabilities is achieved by maintaining the portfolio on the efficient frontier.

The minimum-risk efficient portfolio will match the risk exposures of the assets to those of the liabilities to the extent possible within the given constraints. Those constraints are duration and partial duration, volatility exposure, and exchange-rate exposures. To the extent that a surplus or a deficit exists, dollar-weighting the risk exposures will retain the neutral position.

The minimum risk portfolio will have the following characteristics: First, the total duration of the assets will be matched to the total duration of the liabilities. Additionally, the partial durations at each factor rate will be matched for assets and liabilities, accounting for any potential shifts in different segments of the yield curve. Second, the volatility exposure of the assets and liabilities will be matched. Both assets and liabilities can have a volatility exposure—

that is, some sensitivity to changes in volatility. If exchange rate exposures are present, they too can be matched.

The return associated with the minimum-risk portfolio could be considered the risk-free rate of return for purposes of the asset/liability portfolio. It can be considered risk-free because it is the combination of assets and liabilities that offers the best match of risk exposure between the two and allows the value of the assets to track the value of the liabilities. Given the minimum-risk portfolio as the starting point, advancing up the efficient frontier in terms of higher expected return produces greater mismatches among the risk factors. Thus, the efficient frontier offers a sacrifice of poorer risk exposure matching for higher expected return of assets over liabilities. An appropriate optimizer, using a quadratic programming algorithm, can calculate the minimum-risk portfolio and all the other portfolios along the efficient frontier.

To the extent that the liability composition of a portfolio is discretionary, the weights of the liability classes can be included in the optimization subject to their constraints. So part of the optimization procedure involves identifying optimal liability weights or liability types that may be appropriate for the overall solution. For example, many insurance companies have some flexibility in the liabilities that they assume. In these cases, they could identify specifically what type and how much of those liabilities would provide a more optimal solution.

Conclusion

I have intended to provide a macro overview of a framework for quantifying the various inputs that go into solving for an asset/liability-efficient portfolio. Some elements of this framework can be modified to suit individual circumstances. The critical parts of the analysis are the principles of characterizing assets and liabilities in terms of risk factors and the ability to evaluate those risk factors from the perspective of a full covariance analysis.

The basic formulation of the asset/liability management problem applies equally well either to passive strategies, in which no judgment is made about expected rates of return or changes in the underlying risk factors, or to active strategies, which incorporate the judgments of a manager.

Question and Answer Session

H. Gifford Fong

Question: Does the analysis you discussed change significantly for those people who are constrained by book value accounting on many of the assets?

Fong: Book value accounting imposes an additional constraint in terms of the optimal solution. That would translate into some additional constraints on trading or changing a position in particular assets.

Question: Is the risk of changes in the shape of the yield curve captured in your duration and volatility factors? If not, how do you control this risk?

Fong: The changes in the yield curve are addressed by both the duration and volatility exposure measure. Some of our recent empirical work made use of those two measures. We took the Gulf War period—August 1990 through March 1991—and considered two alternative approaches to an all-Treasury index or index replication. One was a traditional approach of trying to control duration, convexity, and sector concentration. So given the all-Treasury index, we would hold a portfolio that matched the index duration, matched the index convexity, and matched sector concentration as expressed by high–low coupon securities within that index.

In the other approach, we controlled only two factors—duration and volatility exposure. The volatility exposure of any series of cash flows is measurable. So by looking at the index and the individual securities within that index, you can measure the associated volatility exposure.

We then matched the portfolio that we held with the volatility exposure of the index. We compared the results for the three-factor approach with those for the two-factor approach. Over this period, the tracking error of the two-factor approach was about 60 percent lower than that of the three-factor version. Perhaps more important, the standard deviation associated with that tracking error was more than two-thirds smaller for the two-factor approach.

We believe the two most important sources of interest rate change are a basic shift in the level of rates and a change in the associated volatility. Using our two-factor approach, we ended up with a much better portfolio from the standpoint of controlling for interest rate dynamics than a more conventional approach would have given us.

Question: Using your framework, can exposure to credit-risky assets and credit-risky liabilities be incorporated as risk characteristics?

Fong: That would be an additional factor to consider. Our framework does not explicitly account for credit risk, but it could.

Question: Equities were not included in your asset class alternatives in the example. Why was that, and would that change the framework or the results?

Fong: Equities would change the analysis by adding risk factors, but the same principle of considering the correlation in variance of these risk factors would be applicable, and you would end up with an optimal portfolio based upon the relative riskiness of the equities. Now, for a typical asset/liability portfolio, unless the expectation of return for equities is very high, you probably would not incorporate them because you know that the additional risk would be substantial. So in a minimum-risk portfolio, equities would be considered a very risky asset.

Question: How can a bank use the concept of the efficient frontier to enhance income and surplus?

Fong: The constraints government regulation places on the composition of a bank's assets and liabilities sometimes overwhelm the practicalities of implementing these strategies. The relevant constraints should be considered on a case-by-case basis. Sometimes, the constraints are so binding that a particular asset/liability mix is mandatory. The type of analysis I have described is only applicable to the extent that some flexibility exists in the asset mix and potentially in the liability mix.

Question: What hardware and software are required to do this type of optimization, and where can one get it?

Fong: The basic analytical engine behind this analysis is a quadratic programming optimizer. This is in the framework of a traditional mean-variance portfolio optimization problem. Measuring some of the individual risk factors is a bit more complicated. The Fong and Vasicek article in the *Journal of Portfolio Manage-*

ment, which I referenced earlier, describes volatility exposure. Another academic paper, which will provide the formulas for calculating volatility exposure, will be published, probably sometime next year. Our firm provides this service and has an optimization procedure that does it.

Question: How does volatility exposure differ from convexity exposure?

Fong: Duration is the first-order measure of the sensitivity of a security or portfolio to a change in the level of rates; convexity is the second-order measure. Convexity measures the sensitivity of the change in value of duration to changes in rates, so it only deals with the actual shift in rates. It indirectly and only in special cases deals with volatility.

This is perhaps best shown by looking at an actual diagram of the relationship between convexity and term as compared to volatility exposure and term, or maturity. The *Journal of Portfolio Management* article has a diagram showing the relationship between volatility exposure and term. This relationship is quite a bit different from the upward-sloping convex function that you get when you look at convexity.

Allocation Techniques for an Asset/Liability Portfolio

Alfred Weinberger
Director, Bond Portfolio Analysis Group
Salomon Brothers, Inc.

Asset allocation for asset/liability portfolios is a more complex problem than for asset-only situations. Their special constraints can lead to solutions that are different from the market-optimal allocations. Until mark-to-market accounting becomes a reality, it is necessary to find allocations that provide satisfactory compromises between the market and book worlds.

Efficient asset allocations for an asset/liability portfolio will rarely equal those found by considering the assets alone. An asset/liability portfolio is just another way of saying "financial institution"—a bank; an insurance company; and, with a little license, even a pension fund. Much of the asset/liability and asset allocation literature does not address the real-world considerations portfolio managers must contend with in managing the assets of such institutions. Specifically, these institutions are going concerns, not closed blocks of business, and they operate under the burden of institutional and regulatory constraints. For the resulting decisions to be appropriate to the particular needs of each institution, these and other considerations must be included in any analysis. I will illustrate an approach that incorporates real-world issues into the asset allocation decision of a property/casualty insurer, but the basic framework should be applicable to other financial intermediaries.

The Evolution of Asset Allocation Models

Asset allocation models have evolved from an asset-only approach to an asset/liability (i.e., surplus) approach. The traditional asset allocation framework arose from work by Harry Markowitz on the efficient frontier for equity portfolios. **Figure 1** illustrates the Markowitz efficient frontier, which represents the optimal risk/return portfolios achievable. About 20 years ago, the approach was adapted to developing efficient allocations across asset classes.

The prominent characteristic of the early work

was that it centered only on assets. After a while, people realized that asset portfolios do not exist in isolation; they exist to fund liabilities. Optimizing the risk/return for assets deals with only half the problem. The focus should be on the net difference between assets and liabilities, or the surplus.

Later asset allocation models were directed at the surplus, or net worth, of the institutions. The surplus framework is a natural one for such institutions as insurance companies, but even the pension fund community began to think seriously about liabilities and surplus following the passage of FAS No. 87, "Employers' Accounting for Pensions." In a surplus framework, risk is defined as the standard deviation of the return on surplus of the institution rather than the standard deviation of portfolio return. Similarly, return is represented by expected return on surplus.

In the insurance industry, surplus can have meanings other than just the difference between the market value of assets and the market value of liabilities. It can also be measured in two book accounting formats, statutory accounting and generally accepted accounting principles (GAAP) accounting, each of which carries great significance to insurers. Therefore, the asset allocation decision will need to consider financial results in these accounting frameworks, in addition to optimizing the risk/return trade-off for the market value of surplus.

Most of the early work on the surplus framework had a closed-system perspective. It focused on beginning assets and liabilities, without paying attention to the fact that the institution is a going concern. The next step in the evolution was to develop models that incorporated more dynamism. At the end of the decision horizon, the institution is typically different from the characterization in the closed-system analysis. It has paid out some liabilities and taken on new ones with attendant implications for assets as well. Thus, the going-concern perspective focuses on efficient solutions for surplus at the horizon date that include these ongoing flows.

To model that future-date surplus, we need to incorporate what is happening on the operating side. I will use the property/casualty insurance industry to illustrate how this might be done. The size of the property/casualty insurance industry is approximately $500 billion, or one-third the size of the life insurance business. An unfortunate feature of the industry is that it tends to be very cyclical and not very profitable in comparison with other industries. It is a good candidate for trying to improve results, however, which is our objective. Property/casualty insurance comprises personal lines (such as automobile and homeowner's insurance) and commercial lines (such as general liability and worker's compensation). The personal lines are typically known as short-tailed liabilities with durations of one to one-and-a-half years. In contrast, the commercial lines often have durations extending four or five years. Reinsurance companies typically have longer durations as well.

The Model

The purpose of this model is to make efficient asset allocation decisions in a risk/return framework by calculating a mean variance efficient frontier focusing on the company's market value of surplus. The key issues are determining how much stock to own, choosing a duration target for the fixed-income portfolio, and whether to own other asset classes. An

important aspect of the model is that it integrates the business strategies of the company into the asset allocation process. The going-concern framework facilitates this by allowing the manager to determine how such factors as different lines of business and varying degrees of operating leverage affect the optimum asset allocation.

Several adjustments must be made to accommodate an insurance company in an asset allocation framework and to incorporate real-world considerations into the asset allocation process. These include marking the balance sheet to market, modeling the company as a going concern, modeling risk, recognizing regulatory and institutional constraints, and accounting for taxes.

▨ *Marking the balance sheet to market.* Insurance company balance sheets are typically presented in statutory or GAAP terms. For purposes of the model, these must be converted into market value terms. **Figure 2** illustrates the differences between the market and statutory balance sheets of a property/casualty insurer. For this company, marking to market results in a substantially larger surplus than the statutory surplus, because the assets were marked up and the liabilities were reduced. On the asset side, the value of the marked-to-market portfolio is a little larger than the statutory value, because the portfolio has some embedded capital gains.

The equity assets are carried at market value in both cases, so the capital gains are in the fixed-income portfolio. On the liability side, the statutory statements show loss and loss adjustment expense (LAE) reserves and the unearned-premium reserve (UPR). On the market statements, the two reserve categories are combined after an appropriate adjustment to the UPR. The sum of the two represent expected future cash obligations to pay policyholder

Figure 1. The Markowitz Efficient Frontier

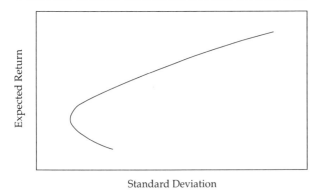

Source: Alfred Weinberger and Vincent Kaminski, "Asset Allocation for Property/Casualty Insurance Companies: A Going-Concern Approach," Salomon Brothers, Inc. (July 1991).

Figure 2. Market versus Statutory Balance Sheet

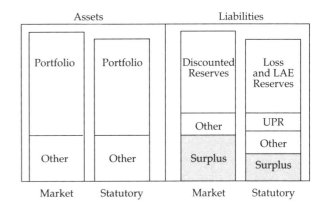

Source: Weinberger and Kaminski, "Asset Allocation for Property/Casualty Insurance Companies."

claims. On a discounted basis, they are a smaller value than the sum of the two undiscounted reserves.

■ *Modeling the company as a going concern.* The going-concern approach allows us to recognize and exploit any correlations between the existing assets and liabilities and the operating cash flows of the company. To the extent that certain economic factors might simultaneously affect starting balance sheet values and the pricing of new liabilities, a model that considers the correlation of these effects will provide a more efficient solution than one that does not.

Another advantage is that the going-concern model can reflect the expected leverage of the horizon balance sheet. Knowing the expected leverage of the balance sheet at the end of the planning horizon allows rational decision making regarding how much risk the company can actually sustain.

Figure 3 illustrates a going-concern model of a property/casualty company, which shows what happens to the balance sheet from the current period (t_0) to the horizon period (t_1). The goal of the model is to find efficient solutions for surplus at time t_1 by making appropriate allocations of the portfolio assets at time t_0.

In Figure 3, the current reserves are split into two components—those that will be paid as cash this year and those that will be paid in future years. The reserves to be paid in the future will undergo changes that will affect their market values. At the end of the time horizon, these reserves are denoted as the old reserves.

The underwriting operations—that is, the premiums collected and the expenses and losses paid during the period—are in the middle of the process. The net cash flow is carried to the end-of-period balance sheet as the net underwriting cash flow. The underwriting operation also generates new liabilities—that is, losses incurred on the business written during the year but not yet paid out as cash by year-end. These are reflected as new reserves on the ending new balance sheet.

The elements of the horizon balance sheet are probabilistic; they are not known with certainty. In other words, each of these elements has its own probability distribution, its own volatility, and its own covariances with the other elements. The mean variance characteristics of surplus will result from the probabilistic addition and subtraction of these elements. The asset decisions at t_0 will affect the surplus distribution because they shape the portfolio

Figure 3. The Dynamics of a Property/Casualty Company

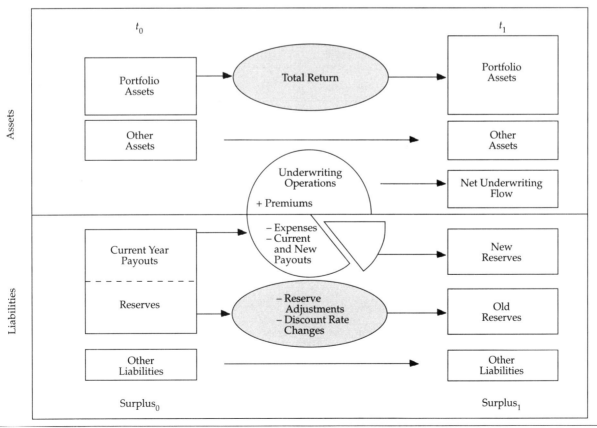

Source: Weinberger and Kaminski, "Asset Allocation for Property/Casualty Insurance Companies."

distribution at time t_1.

■ *Modeling risk.* To combine the horizon balance sheet elements into the surplus probability distribution, we need to determine the covariances among them. The covariance matrix can be estimated using a factor model or by direct computation from historical data. We use the factor model approach in our example. This approach involves regressing each of the asset classes, the net underwriting flow, and the reserve values against a set of common factors. The factors must be related to at least two of the items on the horizon balance sheet; otherwise, they might as well be included in the residual of the regressions—that is, the specific risks. The common macroeconomic factors that we consider and that give rise to the covariances are unexpected changes in interest rates, inflation, and GNP.

Some of the macroeconomic factors, or the factors associated with specific risk, are the actuarial risk of the liabilities, the insurance pricing cycle, and specific asset risks. The actuarial risk of the company's liabilities capture uncertainties such as the difficulty of estimating hurricanes or auto accidents, uncertainties that are largely independent of the macroeconomic factors. The insurance pricing cycle in the property/casualty industry is partly driven by macroeconomics and partly driven by an industry-specific cycle. This latter portion would add specific risk. The specific asset risks capture risks associated with not being totally diversified in the asset portfolios. Thus, the microeconomic factors are those that add risk to only a single item on the balance sheet.

The net effect of including the macroeconomic and microeconomic factors is to characterize the insurer's surplus risk in a total risk framework and not just the interest rate risk framework of the more traditional asset/liability approaches.

■ *Regulatory and institutional constraints.* In the real world, insurance companies cannot focus exclusively on market value maximization. They must also pay attention to regulatory and other institutional constraints, including minimum requirements for such items as statutory surplus, operating earnings, investment income, and cash flow. The model handles these requirements through the imposition of shortfall constraints, which allow the stipulation of a shortfall level and the desired probability for exceeding this level.

To allow these types of constraints, the model must provide for a variety of accounting conventions simultaneously. The combination of a market value maximization objective with "book" value type constraints will often lead to a tug-of-war between the two systems as shown in **Figure 4**, which illustrates the impact of a statutory surplus shortfall constraint on the efficiency of market value surplus.

Allocation A represents an efficient asset allocation with no constraints applied. Panel A1 shows the probability distribution of the horizon market surplus for Allocation A. The resulting probability distribution for statutory surplus with Allocation A is shown in Panel A2. With Allocation A, the probability that statutory surplus will fall below the value S_{min} is 10 percent. If management considers this 10 percent probability too high, the model can be rerun, this time with a shortfall constraint applied to statutory surplus.

Allocation B is the resulting solution when, for example, the shortfall probability is set to 5 percent. As shown in Panel B2, the statutory surplus distribution with Allocation B satisfies the requirement that this surplus should not fall below S_{min} with greater than a 5 percent chance. This constraint, however, has costs in terms of efficiency of market surplus. As shown in Panel B1, the corresponding market surplus probability distribution is less efficient than for Allocation A, because its mean is lower and its variance is unchanged.

■ *Taxes.* Taxes are an additional real-world complication that should be taken into account. In general, asset allocations that are efficient in the pretax case will not necessarily be the most efficient solutions when the effects of taxes are considered. Taxes will affect both the risks and returns of assets and portfolios. The inclusion of taxes into the analysis is a challenging problem. Besides capturing the effects of taxes on income and realized capital gains and losses, an effort must be made to assess the present value of the future tax implications of changes in unrealized gains and losses.

Figure 4. The Impact of a Statutory Surplus Constraint on Market Efficiency

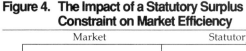
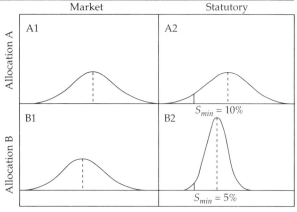

Source: Weinberger and Kaminski, "Asset Allocation for Property/Casualty Insurance Companies."

Case Study

The asset allocation approach can be illustrated with a case study of Sample Property/Casualty Company. The company writes a mix of personal and commercial coverages resulting in a liability duration of about two years. On the asset side, the fixed-income duration is 5.2 years, which is similar to the aggregate for the industry. The current allocation is heavily weighted in fixed-income securities: 82 percent bonds, 12 percent stocks, and 6 percent cash, with expected returns of 10 percent, 14 percent, and 8 percent, respectively.

Figure 5 shows the efficient frontier for this company. Note that the efficient frontier is presented in terms of return on surplus and the standard deviation of return on surplus. In this case, segment D–E is clearly inefficient because it has a lower return and higher risk than allocations on segment E–F. The minimum risk portfolio is E.

Figure 6 shows the allocations among cash, bonds, and stocks for portfolios along the segment D–E–F. The allocation of the minimum-return portfolio, at point D, is entirely cash. In moving to the lowest risk portfolio (point E), we move rather rapidly into bonds. Thus, the most efficient way to reduce risk is to begin to close the duration gap between assets and reserves. The minimum-risk portfolio (portfolio E) is not simply a fixed-income, duration-matched portfolio but contains some small component of stocks. This is not surprising, because the model considers, in addition to interest rates, other common factor sources of risk on the liability side, such as inflation, which may in part be hedged by stocks.

Beyond the minimum risk portfolio, stocks enter the efficient allocations at a rapid rate while the bond weighting continues to increase, albeit at a reduced rate. Thus, the most efficient way to add return at increasing levels of risk is through a diversified portfolio of stocks and bonds and a reduced cash weighting, rather than by just shifting from cash to bonds (i.e., by lengthening the duration of the fixed-income portfolio).

Figure 7 shows the positioning of the company's current portfolio (C) relative to the efficient frontier. More specifically, we highlight the efficient portfolios A and B: A has the same expected return on surplus as the current portfolio but with lower risk, and B has the same risk but with a higher expected return.

Table 1 shows how the current portfolio compares with portfolios A and B. In both cases, the allocation to stocks is much higher than the current 12 percent, and the allocation to bonds is much lower than the current 82 percent. The current portfolio has an expected return on market surplus of 11.1 percent, a standard deviation of 17.3 percent, and a fixed-income duration of 5.2 years. Portfolio A, at the same 11.1 percent return, has a risk of 15.5 percent with a fixed-income duration of 2.7 years. Portfolio B, at the current portfolio's risk of 17.3 percent, has a return of 12.4 percent and a fixed-income duration of 3.2 years. These efficient portfolios have less interest rate risk and more stock risk than the current portfolio.

Although higher weightings in stocks increase the market efficiency of portfolios, most companies have allocations similar to that of Sample Company's current portfolio. The reason for this becomes clear when we consider the performance of the different portfolios expressed in statutory rather than market terms. As shown in Table 1, the statutory return on surplus (operating income divided by statutory sur-

Figure 5. Sample Property/Casualty Company—Unconstrained Efficient Frontier

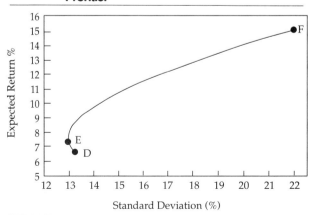

Source: Weinberger and Kaminski, "Asset Allocation for Property/Casualty Insurance Companies."

Figure 6. Sample Property/Casualty Company—Asset Allocation Along the Efficient Frontier

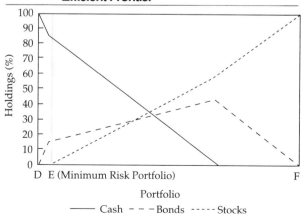

Source: Weinberger and Kaminski, "Asset Allocation for Property/Casualty Insurance Companies."

Table 1. Sample Property/Casualty Company—Aftertax Market and Statutory Results, Current and Efficient Allocations

	Asset			Market			Statutory		
				Return on Surplus		Fixed Income-Duration	Return on Surplus		10% Surplus Risk
Allocation	Cash	Bonds	Stocks	Expected	Deviation	(years)	Expected	Standard Deviation	($millions)
Current	6%	82%	12%	11.1%	17.3%	5.2	9.1%	22.2%	$–29
Allocation A (Return = current)	46	28	26	11.1	15.5	2.7	4.8	22.2	–36
Allocation B (Risk = current)	34	32	34	12.4	17.3	3.2	4.4	22.2	–38

Source: Weinberger and Kaminski, "Asset Allocation for Property/Casualty Insurance Companies."

plus) of 9.1 percent for the current portfolio exceeds by a wide margin the returns of the efficient portfolios, which have the higher concentration of stocks. This is because, for stocks, only the income from dividends is reported as part of statutory operating income and not the capital gains component of return, which represents the major portion of the expected return of stocks. In some cases, realized capital gains may be included in net income, but even then, unrealized capital gains will not flow through statutory income. Rather, unrealized capital gains and losses will affect statutory surplus through "below the line" adjustments.

The standard deviations of statutory returns on surplus for all three portfolios are equal in value. As we have defined statutory income, the only component that contributes variability for reporting purposes is the uncertainty in the company's underwriting results. Each of the investment choices is as-

sumed to produce a predictable flow of income: Cash (with a one-year maturity) will contribute a fixed return, the income component of bonds will be the coupon flow plus known accretions of discount or amortizations of premium, and the dividend component of stocks is assumed to be certain.

The last column of Table 1 contains the 10 percent shortfall values for statutory surplus with each of the asset allocations. For example, for the current portfolio, the chance that statutory surplus will fall by $29 million from year end to year end is 10 percent; for Allocation A, it can fall by $36 million with the same 10 percent probability. These results also tend to disfavor the market efficient portfolios because of their relatively high concentration of stocks and lower bond weightings. This results from accounting conventions for statutory surplus, for which bonds are carried at amortized cost (and therefore appear riskless) but for which stocks are carried

Figure 7. Sample Property/Casualty Company—The Current Portfolio versus Efficient Alternatives

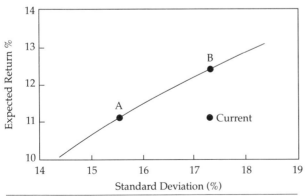

Source: Weinberger and Kaminski, "Asset Allocation for Property/Casualty Insurance Companies."

Figure 8. Sample Property/Casualty Company—Constrained Efficient Frontiers: Various Statutory Surplus Shortfall Levels

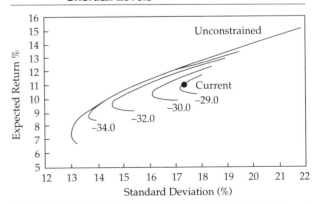

Source: Weinberger and Kaminski, "Asset Allocation for Property/Casualty Insurance Companies."

at market values, thus contributing variability.

Allocations A and B are located on the unconstrained efficient frontier—that is, the frontier found without applying any operating earnings or statutory surplus shortfall constraints. If these allocations are deemed unsatisfactory despite their market efficiency because of the consequences for statutory return on surplus or statutory surplus shortfall risk, other constrained efficient frontiers can be evaluated for suitability and for assessing trade-offs between market optimality and reporting necessity. **Figure 8** displays such constrained frontiers, in this case at various levels of statutory surplus shortfall risk. Each of these frontiers shows the best market risk/return trade-off given the indicated 10 percent shortfall value. These frontiers illustrate the tug-of-war between market and reporting objectives. The best statutory surplus protection shown—$–29 million—provides the least attractive market frontier.

Conclusion

Asset allocation for asset/liability portfolios is a more complex problem than for asset-only situations. Asset/liability portfolios are found in the context of financial institutions that often face constraints on pure market value optimization. In the case of a property/casualty insurer, these constraints can lead to solutions that are quite different from the market-optimal allocations. These constraints result in part from GAAP and statutory accounting conventions that differ from market value accounting. If the recent flurry of proposals regarding mark-to-market accounting materializes into practice in the future, then it will be more feasible for insurers to pursue market-optimal policies. In the meantime, the approach we have discussed can be used to find allocations that provide satisfactory compromises between the market and book worlds.

Question and Answer Session

Alfred Weinberger

Question: To what extent has your work influenced the behavior of insurance companies?

Weinberger: Several companies are using our model, and several others are using the economic approach. I believe interest in the market value, or economic, approach is growing within the industry.

Compared to the current allocations, our models are generating efficient solutions that have considerably greater equity content. This is not an unusual situation for the industry. Just prior to the 1973–74 bear market, property/casualty companies as a group had about 35 percent of their invested assets in equities. Then, because of the bear market, necessity, statutory pressure, or fright, the industry dramatically reduced the allocation to equities. In the late 1970s and early 1980s, interest rates rose, and the industry was hurt by having too high an allocation to long-term, fixed-income securities. That produced the next problem: The companies could not get out of their assets, because selling at a loss reduces statutory surplus. So to attract funds to pay out obligations, the companies did cash flow underwriting; in other words, they priced insurance low enough to attract cash flow, which messed up pricing and reduced returns in succeeding years.

Question: Does this analysis apply to life insurance companies, banks, and thrifts?

Weinberger: Yes, it applies to all types of financial institutions. For example, the biggest influence on life insurance companies' assets is probably interest rates. The same is true on the liability side, at least for balance sheet liabilities. It would be interesting to investigate how pricing and amounts of new business might be influenced by various factors such as GNP. Incorporating new business as part of the analysis might produce some interesting new dimensions. Even if only interest rates are considered on the liability side, the companies are not necessarily going to operate on a risk-free basis. So they go ahead and match with interest rate instruments until the duration gap is closed. Now, if they want to take risk, which is the best way to move from that point forward?

What was illustrated here would apply to any institution. Why take on a bigger interest rate mismatch when some diversification benefits are possible? The interest rate bets are already covered on the liability side. Everything extra is in an asset-only framework, in which diversification in some sense is desirable. This is particularly true for a life insurance company, because the only influence on liabilities is interest rates. Once that is covered, why not have a diversified portfolio of assets?

Asset and Liability Modeling in the Insurance Industry—Part I: Liability Management

Jack L. Gibson
Consulting Actuary
Coopers & Lybrand

Insurance companies typically have a broad array of liabilities, and the risks of these liabilities are affected by external factors including changes in interest rates, the economic cycle, the distribution system, competition, and sales volume.

Certain liabilities, including many life insurance liabilities, are too complex to allow for the direct application of the various sophisticated theories and formula-based calculations in asset/liability modeling. I will review and compare various liabilities for insurance companies and then discuss the management of the more-complex life insurance liabilities. Bob Matczak will discuss asset/liability modeling.[1] We will also discuss outside influences that can have a significant impact on asset/liability management decisions.

Comparison of Liability Types

The types of financial liabilities vary across industries. Insurance companies typically have a broader array of liabilities than other financial institutions.

Life Insurance

Life insurance companies have four basic types of liabilities: traditional life, interest-sensitive life, variable life, and annuities. In traditional life, the premium charges a company imposes are typically based on a "worst case" scenario so that no matter what happens to interest rates or expected mortality, the company will have enough money on hand to pay its obligations. The company's actual experience is paid back retrospectively in the form of dividends to policyholders.

Life insurance companies also offer interest-sensitive life insurance, a good example being universal life. With this type of insurance, the actual experience is paid back immediately in the form of lower

cost of insurance charges and higher credited interest rates applied to the account value fund. Universal life generally offers additional contract flexibility and, most significantly, premium flexibility. This flexibility adds a lot to the risk an insurer takes. It gives policyholders the ability to antiselect against the company when the company's credited interest rate is lower than the rates available in the external market or for other reasons.

Another type of policy, variable life insurance, is one way insurers have tried to transfer particular investment risks to the policyholders by allowing insureds to select how their money is invested and applying the resultant investment results, less a spread, to the account value.

Finally, annuities are liabilities that tend to be more directly linked to assets. They can have life contingencies attached to them, or they can be purely nonlife contingent annuities. They look more like negative assets and are much easier to model than the other liabilities. That is why single-premium deferred annuities and similar types of liabilities are typically used in theoretical analysis.

Property/Casualty

Property/casualty insurance liabilities have a shorter duration than life policies, typically one year. As a result, the interest rate risk is minimal. Nevertheless, the property/casualty industry faces significant and, in some cases, profound risks of other types. Geographic risk is one example, and the industry obviously has some very strong regulatory constraints and pressures from California and other states as well.

---

[1]See Mr. Matczak's presentation, pp. 33–36.

Noninsurance

Noninsurance financial liabilities tend to be less complicated. Like annuities, they are easier to think of as a negative asset, and a theoretical-based approach to active asset/liability management is more applicable to these liabilities. My remaining comments will be directed toward the more-complex insurance liability risks that cannot be successfully modeled using existing simplified techniques.

Insurance Liability Risks

Insurance liability risks are affected by a variety of external and company-specific factors, including changes in interest rates, the economic cycle, the distribution system, competition, and sales volume.

Changes in Interest Rates

If the market interest rate goes up, and a company has an existing universal life contract with assets invested longer than the liabilities, it will have a problem. If the company leaves its credited interest rate that is applied to the account value fund at its present level, it will see increased policy lapses, increased policy loan utilization, and a decrease in discretionary premiums. All of these actions will increase net cash outflow and produce a demand for assets. Obviously, the converse case occurs when the market rate drops.

The Economic Cycle

Interest rate changes are related to swings in the economic cycle. Inflation and recession can cause problems with expense levels and sales volume. Also, age demographics, such as the aging of the baby boomers, can affect the characteristics of the insurance market and what types of products will be of interest.

The Distribution System

There are four primary distribution systems: agent/general agent, brokerage, direct-response, and other. The principal category is the career agency system. An agent solely representing one company and selling all of its products is becoming less typical. When this is the case, however, the agent has a certain amount of loyalty to the company. With loyalty, however, comes the company need to offer multiple lines of insurance, even though some of those lines may not be profitable. The problem a career agency company faces is having a fairly significant amount of fixed expenses that must be spread across a very large sales base.

In the brokerage market, an insurance company's expenses tend to be much more variable than fixed, but company loyalty is lacking. As a result, any product offered for sale in a brokerage environment must be competitive. If the insurance company down the street is a little meaner and leaner, its products will do well in a brokerage environment. Companies have to find a way to cut profits and/or manage their expenses and risks better to be able to sell a lower priced product.

The direct-response insurance business has a different compensation structure and its own share of risks. Another competitive threat is the movement of insurance products into the banking industry. Each of these needs to be analyzed in its own right to determine the inherent risks.

Interest-Crediting Strategy

Competitive forces drive many risks in the insurance industry. The interest-crediting strategy in interest-sensitive products is a very difficult problem. If a company has assets that are longer than its liabilities and interest rates go up, should it raise its interest-crediting rate to follow the market (and keep its policy lapses low), or should it keep a fixed interest spread to try to maintain its profitability? If it keeps a fixed spread and lapses increase, profitability can go down anyway. These are the two obvious strategy extremes, but no company does only one or the other. Most companies probably tend to follow the market but say that they are fixing the spread.

Dividend and participating traditional life insurance increasingly resembles interest-sensitive insurance. In theory, the company can pass along its problems—such as a decrease in earned interest rates or adverse mortality experience—to its policyholders through dividend policy. In practice, however, insurance companies are finding it difficult to do so. For example, if a company has had a notably bad experience with defaults because of the way it has invested, but its competitors are not invested in quite the same way, it will have a difficult time passing along that experience and remaining competitive. The company may have to absorb the defaults.

Policy provisions present two different categories of risk. One is that marketing will emphasize certain key characteristics instead of the overall performance of the product. A good example is the credited interest rate. With universal life contracts, the focus sometimes is so one-minded on the credited interest rate that all the profitability comes, not from the policy itself, but from peripheral sources such as cost of insurance charges, expense charges, and the like. With the flexibility of universal life contracts, anytime a company's charges are mismatched against the way the money flows in, the policyholder can antiselect against that company. If the company puts a small amount of its profitability into its interest rate component and a large amount into its cost of insurance component, it will attract premium-intensive contractholders and end up being less profitable than it had expected.

Surrender charges are another policy provision that is a source of risk. For example, in the early stages of the guaranteed investment contracts (GIC) market, competitive pressures forced companies to offer very lucrative and ultimately damaging options in the form of pour-in provisions, which allowed for the investment of future premiums at the existing contract interest rate. These market pressures and the fact that many people followed companies such as the Equitable led to the downfall of many GIC portfolios.

Market diversity can be a significant problem in a career agency system. For example, the annual renewable term market is very competitive, and many companies believe they need to offer their agents the capability to sell term insurance and to offer a competitive product. Substandard issues are difficult to price profitably, except in great volume, but companies feel a need to offer such services to their agency forces.

Another risk item driven by competitive forces is nonlevel commissions. Commissions on insurance products are very much weighted toward the early years after a contract is sold, which poses considerable risk for the companies. Some regulations in the state of New York impede the ability of companies to have level commissions, and the competition for agents also discourages a company from going to a level-commission system. If the whole industry made the switch at once, the agents would be likely to accept it.

Sales Volume

Another key risk area in today's environment is developing critical mass—a company's need to spread its fixed expenses across a larger sales volume. Many companies, in their pricing, assume that with increased sales volume and a decrease in unit expenses they can price their product to attract sales and still be profitable. These increased sales pressures can cause problems, however. Typically, the pressure on the sales force to make the sales at all costs may lead them to sell "bad business"—sales to policyholders that are not really sure that this is what they want to do with their money and whose policies eventually lapse. Also, if underwriting standards are relaxed in an attempt to increase sales, a level of claims that was not assumed in the pricing may occur; for example, in a disability product, the

company's mortality or morbidity experience could deteriorate.

The result of this stressing of critical mass has been a strong increase in mergers, acquisitions, and demutualization. One notable example is Equitable, which already has a board resolution and is well into the demutualization process. Other companies are also trying to find a way to address this expense issue.

These are certainly not all the risks insurance companies face, but they are some of the key factors that affect insurance liability risks, both from an investment perspective and from other perspectives.

Duration and Convexity

One notable characteristic of life insurance liabilities is that they have durations longer than most assets, which can present problems. Furthermore, because of the relationship of the interest rate to the market value of policies, the liabilities tend to have a positive convexity. As interest rates increase, policy lapse rates and policy loan utilization will increase, causing concavity in the liabilities. In contrast, because of the call provisions of bonds, mortgage prepayments, and so forth, insurance company assets have a negative convexity.

Figure 1 is a fairly typical diagram of an insurance company's product that was priced in the then-current interest rate environment at a level that would be the most profitable. If interest rates move in either direction, because of the difference in the

Figure 1. Duration and Convexity, Insurance Company Product

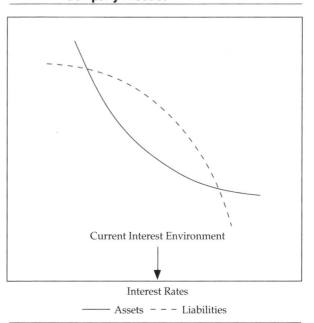

Current Interest Environment

Interest Rates

——— Assets – – – Liabilities

convexity of the liabilities and the assets, the profitability of the product declines and, depending on the product's characteristics and the way the company's assets are invested, the band of interest rates in which the product is profitable at all can be fairly small. This is a serious problem that needs to be addressed.

Management of Life Insurance Liabilities

An interest-crediting strategy is one way a company can manage its liabilities. The two extreme strategies are fixing the interest spread and following the market, and the choice of strategy is strongly influenced by competitive forces.

A second way to manage liabilities is with persistency bonuses. Any agents that have a pattern of selling persistent business could be rewarded with an enhanced commission so they have an incentive to sell the better business.

Paying persistency bonuses to policyholders is also gaining favor. These bonuses can be for persistency by duration (e.g., if policyholders last until the 10th or 15th year, they get a boost in their interest rate) or for high premiums. Sometimes companies will realize that the real risk lies in the premium flexibility they have given policyholders in these interest-sensitive products. As a result, the companies put in tiered interest rates or other features that allow them to push policyholders gently in a favor-

able direction from a risk perspective.

Dividend philosophy is gaining a resemblance to interest-sensitive products as companies link interest rates to dividends and also because of the direct recognition of policy loans. Variable loan rates have also allowed companies to manage the policy-loan problem and make it less of a risk factor.

Pricing policy can help deal with a lot of these liability issues effectively before the insurance contract is written. For interest-sensitive life insurance, if the risks are per-policy types of risks, an expense charge should cover the per-policy expense. If the risks are associated with mortality flow, more should be charged for cost of insurance. These are ways to effectively insulate the company against policyholder antiselection by using the flexibility of the contract. Companies have battled the unprofitability of early lapse by imposing higher surrender charges. Because of the heaped commissions and high underwriting expenses, having negative cash values at early durations would be desirable, but you cannot do that.

A general rule of thumb is that the key to effective pricing of liabilities is to decrease the policyholder's opportunity to antiselect. Another way to alter the convexity of the liability curve is to design and sell products with offsetting risk characteristics. If sold in the right proportions, this is a way to manage mismatch as well.

Asset and Liability Modeling in the Insurance Industry—Part II: Modeling Considerations

Robert J. Matczak
Consulting Actuary
Coopers & Lybrand

The use of asset/liability modeling by the insurance industry continues to expand because it is useful in analyzing several critical aspects of insurance company management. The asset and the liabilty sides of the model are governed by different considerations, and the implications of outside influences differ as well.

I will discuss the uses of asset/liability modeling from the perspective of life insurance companies. I will take a macro approach and look at a company's entire asset/liability portfolio. I will then turn to the considerations in modeling liabilities and briefly discuss the considerations in modeling assets. My perspective with regard to the asset/liability modeling process itself is one of classic risk analysis, particularly the notion of the valuation actuary.

Uses for Asset/Liability Modeling

Asset/liability modeling has several uses, including in risk analysis, analysis of interest rate crediting strategies, analysis of investment strategies, merger and acquisition work, and strategic planning.

Risk Analysis

Risk analysis is typically performed by a valuation actuary to meet reserve adequacy requirements. The life insurance industry is regulated by state insurance departments. Even though state laws are similar, they are also unique. New York Regulation 126 was the first to force actuaries dealing with interest-sensitive annuity products—such as single-premium deferred annuities, flexible premium and deferred annuities, guarantee and investment contracts (GIC), and other group annuities—to perform cash flow tests showing that the margins priced into the products are sufficient to pay the benefits. That regulatory framework is being expanded: For products such as universal life, single-premium whole life, and traditional life insurance, the actuary must cer-

tify that the reserves together with the backing assets are sufficient to pay the benefits to the policyholders.

Risk analysis may also be conducted to determine target or required surplus levels. The same valuation actuary will not only provide assurance that reserves are adequate but also determine the level of surplus a company should be holding or targeting in its pricing margins to back up its risks on both sides of the balance sheet. I refer to this as target or required surplus.

In addition, risk analysis can be used to estimate a company's viability. The valuation actuary can perform projections to determine the ability of the company to withstand risks under alternate interest rate or economic scenarios, to pay benefits, and to be able to grow—that is, its ability to put new business on the books, expand its agency force, and do what is necessary to be competitive in the industry.

Other Uses

Asset/liability models are also used to evaluate interest-crediting strategies and their associated risks and investment strategies.

We use asset/liability modeling in rehabilitation and in merger and acquisition work. Just three or four years ago, our strategic planning and merger work would not go into detail on the asset side. We would focus on liabilities and make some assumptions about interest rate spreads that would be earned on interest-sensitive products and about whether the assets would be sufficient to back the dividend scale on traditional life. Then, we incorporated factors such as expenses and mortality.

As has become apparent from the companies that have had problems and those that have come under scrutiny for the types of asset portfolios they are holding, strategic planning and merger and acquisition work require modeling the asset side of the balance sheet on a detailed level and modeling the cash flow and liquidity positions of the company together with its liabilities.

Modeling Considerations for Liabilities

A number of factors impact the cash flow in and out of a company's products and hence its liabilities. With interest-sensitive products, such as universal life and deferred annuities, a company's interest rate crediting strategy is critical. Should it follow the market, try to continue to earn its spread, or pursue some combination of both? That decision requires some assumptions about policy lapses and surrenders. If the company tries to maintain its spread, it will always earn a margin. But how long will business survive if the interest rate the company pays begins to move away from competitive market rates?

Another critical assumption is the level of premium payments for flexible-premium plans, in which premium payments are not required to keep a policy in force. This level will vary as the company's interest rate crediting moves with changes in the overall economic environment, as will utilization rates on policy loans and other options that may be available on the product the company is selling. The company's experiences will differ under different interest rate and economic scenarios. The company also must make assumptions about what its mortality experience and its expenses will be.

For traditional life products, the dividend scale philosophy is important. When a mutual company decides on the dividend to pay back to policyholders as its experience emerges, it assumes a certain level of earnings. As time passes, and if earnings go above the level assumed, it can increase the dividend and raise that assumed earnings rate. Historically, insurance companies lumped all of their traditional life policyholders in one big portfolio so that everyone's dividend was based on the same earnings rate. The policyholders who came in during the 1950s, 1960s, and 1970s would be lumped with the people who came in the 1990s. If a company had older assets that were still earning low interest rates, everyone would be affected.

To increase their competitiveness and keep their dividend scale more competitive relative to products such as universal life, many companies have moved away from lumping all policyholders together. Instead, they have begun to cordon off their investment portfolios, even for their traditional life business, and create investment generations. As interest rates change, a company cordons off a portfolio that will have an effective dividend scale of its own; newer policyholders will get a dividend scale based upon a different interest rate than older policyholders.

The result is increased pressure on companies to be able to sustain that dividend. Historically, the dividend scales were priced very conservatively, with low interest rates that companies knew were attainable. The competitive marketplace does not allow that anymore, so the margins priced into dividends are much thinner. This places pressure on the companies and on the valuation actuaries to continue supporting this dividend scale as interest rates change. Again, the answer to that is affected not only by interest rate movements, but also by movements in the asset side of the balance sheet.

Traditional life policies once had a feature called "fixed policy loan interest rates." A policyholder could borrow against such a policy at a 6 percent or 8 percent interest rate. If gross investment rates available in the market place are higher, say 14 percent, being able to borrow at 6 percent or 8 percent is an attractive option. Many companies were burned on that option in the late 1970s and early 1980s, when interest rates were high. To protect themselves, they developed "direct recognition," which involves adjusting the dividend for differences between the policy loan interest rate and the current market rate in the event the current market rate is higher than the policy loan rate.

Another way of handling this risk is through variable loans. Rather than fixing the policy loan rates, the companies establish a variable-rate option in the life insurance contract by charging the current rate for policy loans.

Other liabilities, such as GIC and group and individual payout annuities, present an easier modeling problem because once the business is on the books, those liabilities are fixed. The insurance company knows exactly what its GIC payments will be and can predict fairly accurately what its payments will be on a payout annuity. The risk here is more a pricing risk at the time the business is put on the books. Are the asset risks adequately priced? The interest rate used to price the product is what makes or breaks a company in terms of competitiveness. Some of these contracts are long-term liabilities, so companies are taking significant risks on what they can earn. In many cases, the contracts are also based on a spot rate. Companies have developed problems with these types of fixed liabilities by inadequately pricing the risks on the assets that back the products.

Modeling Considerations for Assets

Modeling considerations for assets can be separated into two types—basic and advanced. The basic considerations are yield rates, coupon rates, maturity dates, and so forth, which are used to project the basic cash flows of the assets. The advanced considerations are calls and prepayments, defaults and foreclosures, collateralized mortgage obligations, and non-fixed-income issues. The model should reflect the different behavior of these considerations in different interest environments.

Consideration of potential defaults on bonds and foreclosures on mortgages of insurance companies is critical in today's environment. The notion and evolution of asset/liability modeling and the regulatory concern have arisen because of the problems insurance companies had with interest rate risks in the late 1970s and early 1980s.

The problems companies are having today are with asset quality, not with duration mismatch. We have been in a relatively flat or steadily declining interest environment recently. In late 1990 and early 1991, Executive Life had problems with high-yield bonds—the deterioration of the market and defaults on the assets. The company had a lot of fixed liabilities on its books that were priced aggressively (so as to pass on most of the earnings on the high-yield bonds to policyholders rather than putting the earnings aside as a cushion in case the bonds deteriorated).

The concern now is for insurance companies that are heavily concentrated in mortgages and real estate. Because of the current recession, many companies are having foreclosures on their mortgage portfolio and a lot of liquidity problems. When we do our modeling now, real estate is a critical item and one that comes under close scrutiny.

Other Considerations

Several overall issues must be considered as well. First, in a macro approach to modeling, assets and liabilities must be viewed together. Second, different interest rate scenarios must be considered. Interest rate scenarios are a topic in themselves. How do you derive interest rate scenarios? How many should be run if you are doing a risk analysis based on changes in interest rates? Third, results must be evaluated.

We use sensitivity analysis, because in the type of work we are doing now, there are no absolutes. We rarely run only one scenario, whether it is for a rehabilitation plan for a company having problems, a potential merger situation, or a company asset/liability cash flow study. We run multiple scenarios looking at alter-

nate assumptions for all the variables in the model. The alternative default and foreclosure assumptions on the asset side are particularly important variables to do sensitivity on. The results of sensitivity analysis allow us to present both the optimistic and the pessimistic view of the company.

Outside Influences

Outside influences affect companies' asset/liability models, their strategic planning, and the overall view on business. First, the regulations that govern the industry are changing. For example, under evolving legislation, companies cannot model just their universal life portfolios or their deferred annuity portfolios; they will have to do a cash flow analysis for the entire company.

Second, actuarial standards of practice now require actuaries to do cash flow testing in virtually all work, whether it is strategic planning, financial projections, product pricing, or devising a reserving methodology. From a regulatory standpoint, the action of some states in taking over insurance companies is a wake-up call for many other state insurance departments, which are now looking more closely at the companies under their jurisdiction. They are examining balance sheets and are more likely to put companies that raise concerns on call. They are also doing more research into the financial stability and outlook for specific companies. This is creating pressure for the companies themselves, because regulators now have a keener sense of what is going on.

Rating agencies such as Standard & Poor's and Moody's have a critical impact on the industry. Many companies are being downgraded as a result of two things. First, the rating agencies themselves are, to a certain extent, repositioning the ratings of companies. Five years ago, if a company did not get an Aaa rating, it was assumed to have major problems. As the rating agencies began to do a better job of looking at companies, they began to assign a full distribution of ratings for companies. Even today, however, most companies are rated Aaa, Aa, or A. Very few are in the Baa category, which would still be considered a sound investment by most standards. For an insurance company to be rated Baa now is to have a bad rating and to cause regulators, policyholders, and contractholders to wonder why.

I think ratings will continue to come down to give a better distribution across the various ratings, and some unfortunate companies will be downgraded only because of this correction. Other companies are being hit with rightfully deserved downgrades because their conditions have deteriorated. Contractholders who see that their insurance company was downgraded three times in the past 12 months—particularly group pension contractholders with large sums of money in a company—will be deeply concerned, even if the first two downgrades were the result of a correction in the rating system and only the third was truly deserved. After what happened with Executive Life and in cases in which some group pension plans were burned, a pension trustee with money invested in an insurance company will be very concerned and asking lots of questions.

Today, rating agencies pepper insurance companies with questions about what their asset portfolios look like; how their assets relate to their liabilities; and how much of their assets are in risky investments, such as mortgages and real estate, relative to

their surplus levels. So the rating agencies are helping policyholders and in the long run will be effective in letting policyholders and companies deal with these issues. Currently, however, they are creating mush pressure for insurance companies to respond to their concerns.

Auditors also influence the industry. Auditors typically would be concerned about making sure that all of the accounts' debits and credits balance and that the actuaries use the right mortality tables and interest rates. Now auditors must also be concerned about balance sheet issues. They have to look at the cash flow testing generated by internal cash flow actuaries. If the insurance company is not aware of these issues and is not doing this testing, auditors must make sure they do.

Question and Answer Session

Jack L. Gibson
Robert J. Matczak

Question: Please discuss the use of modeling techniques for asset/liability matching for use in pricing life insurance to the consumer. Is this step ignored?

Gibson: Asset/liability matching has been ignored in the past, but changes in the regulations are requiring companies to take note of it. Models are difficult to apply to pricing because they deal with a hypothetical investment portfolio. Sometimes the model can be so simplistic that it does not present a realistic picture of what the problems will be, but it can at least help identify the issues.

Question: Is your firm prepared to attest to the market value of insurance companies' liabilities?

Gibson: The market value of liabilities is difficult to define, but we address this problem by testing different scenarios, based on an analysis in which the assets and liabilities are integrated. A classic case of the need to determine market value liabilities arose with the demutualization of Equitable. The need was to identify the assets to be set aside to fund the future benefits to be provided to the existing participating policyholders and pay their future dividend scales. The assets needed to provide for these benefits are essentially equal to the market value of the liabilities for these participating contracts.

Matczak: We had to calculate the market value of liabilities and assets for Executive Life in 1991. The first step was to recognize that the assets would not generate the expected cash flows. Given the deficiencies in the asset portfolio, what could Executive Life afford to pay its contractholders? To answer that, we had to determine what cash flows were going to be on the liabilities and how much money was owed to the policyholders. We determined that the market value of the liabilities exceeded that of the assets by between 25 and 30 percent.

Question: How would you place a value on a defaulted insurance company product such as a GIC with Executive Life when measuring the asset/liability relationship of an ongoing entity such as a pension fund?

Matczak: The Executive Life situation is still not settled because of some special litigation, so it is too early to tell what exactly will happen. In Executive Life's case, the interest rates being credited, as well as the amount of the liability itself, have been downgraded lower. Certainly an Executive Life GIC is worth a lot less today than it was 12 months ago. It is going to vary in each case depending on what level of interest rates they come out with.

There are special GICs issued to nonpension plans that threw a monkey wrench into the whole situation. Originally, California insurance departments said that the GICs issued to municipalities—funding agreements—were not in the same class as all of the other insurance and annuity contracts of Executive Life. Therefore, they may be paid 25 cents on the dollar. A judge just overruled that two weeks ago so that all the GIC contractholders are in the same class.

Question: If we had true market value accounting for assets and liabilities effectively able to market value both sides of the balance sheet, would Regulation 126 certification still be necessary?

Matczak: Yes. The market values of both would be different under the various scenarios and, most important, the relationships between the market value assets relative to the liabilities. Regulation 126 in essence requires market value accounting in that you have to project forward and run off the assets and liabilities and see what you have left. The present value of the projected cash flow is akin to calculating a market value.

Managing Surplus

Thomas E. Messmore, CFA[1]
Senior Vice President
The Travelers Insurance Company

Investment practitioners are beginning to view assets and liabilities not as independent notions but as interrelated concepts to be managed in a coordinated fashion. One proposal is to create an "obligatory asset liability" swap to enable market value accounting for unmarketable assets and liabilities, motivate managements to report fair market value as best they can, and allow intermediaries to maintain relationships with customers on both the asset and the liability sides.

Managing surplus is a relevant and important topic for financial intermediaries—the institutions whose function is to stand between the sources and uses of wealth in our economy. Financial institutions collect assets from those with wealth, creating corresponding liabilities in the process, and invest those assets in the users of funds. The excuses, means, and labels for collecting the assets or generating liabilities vary, sometimes more as a function of local or national law than from any real economic cause, and the shingle on the door is determined as much by management choice, expertise, and choice of regulatory domain as anything else. I assert for convenience, if not for complete accuracy, that financial intermediaries are more similar than different. Thus, managing surplus is a generic topic, applicable to banks, savings and loans, insurance companies, pension funds, mutual funds, and other forms of financial intermediaries.

Technically, the term "managing surplus" is misnamed, because surplus is a regulatory accounting concept and, under current rules and conventions, a flawed one. Managing net worth is a far better term. Throughout this presentation, I use the terms surplus and net worth almost interchangeably.

Evolution of Asset/Liability Management

Most financial intermediaries started with a focus on the liability side of the balance sheet and were nurtured primarily by people with unique talent and distinguishing expertise on the liability-generation

side. Some might call this the asset-collection side. For example, most insurance companies were created and managed by talented actuaries and marketing people rather than by distinguished investors, with the exception, perhaps, of Warren Buffett. This remains the case today. Actuaries, marketing people, and lawyers dominate the senior leadership positions at many insurance companies. Similar examples are found in the banking and savings and loan businesses; similarly, the exceptions, such as J.P. Morgan, are more notable in their rarity than in their ubiquity.

For most of the 20th century and for most of the financial intermediaries, the key to success was to manage and market the liability side effectively and avoid mistakes on the asset side. Three compelling pieces of evidence support this view: the accounting rules, the regulatory process, and the extant asset mixes. If developed, these pieces of evidence would prove this has been a liability-driven process for most of the century. The buy-and-hold mentality with low risks—at least under the concepts of risk captured by the accounting and regulatory process—has dominated the investing side of financial intermediaries for most of the century.

Only in the past few decades has meaningful progress taken place on managing the asset side. During the 1980s, companies began to manage the asset side using now familiar concepts: total return, modern portfolio theory, mean-variance analysis, and so forth.

Unfortunately, most of the attempts at improving asset management are still forced to fit into the accounting rules and regulatory constructs of an ear-

---

[1]The views expressed herein are those of the author and do not necessarily represent the views of the Travelers companies.

lier, inconsistent, and outmoded liability-oriented paradigm. Nevertheless, irreversible progress is under way.

Now we are beginning to see the liability side and the asset side not as two separate and independent concepts but as two intimately related and interrelated concepts that should be managed in a coordinated and integrated fashion. The concept is becoming clear, and its merits are indisputable. Tools are being developed, the body of skill and expertise is building rapidly, and the evolution is nearly complete.

Necessary Conditions

Three conditions are necessary for true asset/liability management. First, we need a greater theoretical understanding of the asset/liability management concept.

Second, we need greater understanding of the asset/liability management concept on an applied basis by company managements, regulators, and investors. Assets cannot be artificially segregated into distinct piles—some for policyholders and some for shareholders—because cash flows and money are fungible concepts. Managements (and regulators) need to understand that every asset and liability on the balance sheet can be decomposed into a stream of cash flows—some in, some out, some big, some small, some short, some long, some probable, and some certain. The picture of an aggregate net cash flow stream of immense complexity with funds flowing from the providers to the users and back again is increasingly recognized as the real nature of the financial intermediary business. Making as much money as possible while the intermediary has the funds, while providing safe coverage of the liabilities and providing for future growth, is the key to financial success in the financial intermediary business.

Third, accounting standards need to be changed to allow/require assets and liabilities to be treated consistently and in a fashion that enables correct risk analysis and comparison. We need to change from the historical amortized-cost basis for assets to an accounting concept that recognizes real values and the potential for change. Accounting should reflect the true values and the true risks of our investments, both on the asset and on the liability sides of the balance sheet. As *Business Week* magazine recommended, "Let's rip away insurers' accounting fiction that assets never vary in price" (July 8, 1991). In this regard, the Securities and Exchange Commission (SEC), in its efforts to bring about market value accounting, should do so in a manner that is consistent for assets *and* liabilities. Failing to do so may only

make matters worse.

Under book value accounting in the insurance industry, most assets are carried at historical cost, and most liabilities are carried at estimated undiscounted future value. (Worker's compensation is a notable exception on the property/casualty side, in that these reserves are generally discounted.) These monetary values from different time periods cannot be combined in any meaningful way to determine the current net worth of the firm. Under current rules, the net worth shown on a balance sheet does not have much meaning; it is merely an unquantified mix of past and future values. Only in the special case in which interest rates are zero and never change can amortized historical book cost for assets and undiscounted future values for liabilities be added and subtracted with meaning.

The price–book-value ratios of insurance companies that changed hands in recent decades illustrate this point. Ratios of 1.5 to 2.5, which were typical enough to become rules of thumb, indicate how much correction was necessary to the audited financial statements to arrive at fair value for net worth in real transactions. This thought cannot be comforting to any accountant, auditor, or regulator who approved financial statements stating that they fairly represented the financial condition of the firm when the marketplace says that they are as much as 50 percent to 100 percent wrong.

Book value accounting is largely misunderstood. It systematically understates risk and in my judgment has caused more problems for financial intermediaries than most people appreciate. This occurs because book value accounting does not allow risks to show up in financial statements until after the potential risk (credit or interest rate or other risks) has occurred and been realized. In my opinion, book value accounting was largely responsible for the mismatch risk that caused the massive problems in the savings and loan (S&L) industry. Without book value accounting, the S&L industry never would have borrowed so short and lent so long in such a leveraged fashion with book value capital ratios below 3 percent. I also feel book value accounting is largely responsible for banks and insurance companies taking excessive credit and illiquidity risks in the never-ending quest for book yield.

Because book value accounting does not allow or require assets or liabilities to be carried at fair current value, it does not serve us well in the asset/liability management of businesses and investment processes. If evolution to real asset/liability management is to continue, we must enable accounting and regulatory rules to catch up with the economic realities of the world. Unless we change accounting rules, parts of our industry will remain at a competitive disadvantage, which means that the evolution of the industry will stop.

Although accounting methods are clearly not the only difference, it is nevertheless interesting to analyze the relative growth rates of mutual funds (which use market value accounting) and banks, S&Ls, and insurance companies (which use book value accounting) during the past decade. The competitive realities and systematic advantages and disadvantages speak for themselves.

Despite the advantages of market value accounting, the change from book value accounting will not be easy. In fact, the transition will be very difficult and require adjustments by all players. The transition should be managed carefully and gradually during a time of relative financial stability by responsible industry professionals rather than risking political intervention in a time of financial turmoil.

Objections to Market Value Accounting

Market value accounting is alleged to raise many problems, but the criticisms do not hold up, in my view, under careful analysis. The biggest ones are these:

Prices are not directly observable, especially for unlisted and untraded assets and liabilities. The industry prices untraded assets and liabilities every day and is willing to trade on those values. The lack of observability is more a problem for the accountants and auditors than for the participants and stakeholders.

Market values require judgment and subjectivity for untraded assets and liabilities. What is wrong with judgment and subjectivity? Professional judgment is better than an objective number that is nonjudgmental but demonstrably wrong.

Market values change too much; they are too volatile. Of course things change; such variables as interest rates, spreads, real estate market levels, inflation, and systematic risks all change. Pretending that they do not on the accounting statements does not remove the risk that they will change. A major problem with book value accounting is that it denies that these changes occur.

Market values are not under management's control. Of course not all financial results of an economic operation are under management control. This problem springs from confusion about the use of financial statements to measure management performance as opposed to the economic condition of the enterprise.

The industry lacks the tools and expertise necessary to assess value. If the industry lacks the tools to value assets and liabilities, it should not be buying and selling assets and liabilities. Financial intermediaries are uniquely well equipped because they employ people capable of valuing assets and liabilities; they do so every day. Furthermore, services to help perform these functions are available for a small fee.

Market value accounting is too expensive. To the contrary, what is expensive is not knowing the market value of assets and liabilities. Witness the cost to the industry and to society of the S&L debacle.

In my judgment, Business Week and SEC Chairman Richard C. Breeden are correct in advocating that financial intermediaries evolve toward an accounting and regulatory system based upon fair or market or present value—or concepts closely linked thereto. In a free market economy, I know of no better means of assessing value of assets or liabilities, and therefore their difference—that is, surplus or net worth—than by using the collective wisdom of all investors to establish fair market values for both assets and liabilities. Disclosure is not enough; regulatory rules, rating agency ratios, and management decisions are all linked to the reported numbers. The collective wisdom of an entire market may be imprecise, may be difficult to measure or determine, and may appear to be wrong for a period of time, but in the final analysis, the market is a better judge of value than any other arbitrary value imposed by an accountant, actuary, auditor, or regulatory body.

The Obligatory Asset/Liability Swap

To help address the fairness or objectivity issue and motivate an unbiased valuation process, I propose a new asset type be created. This asset would enable true market value accounting for unmarketable assets and liabilities, motivate managements to report fair market values with the best judgment they can apply, and allow intermediaries to maintain valued relationships with their customers on both the asset and the liability sides. In addition, it would enlist the entire market, especially one's competitors, as disciplinarians to assess values and prevent massive or systematic cheating. I call this proposed asset type the obligatory asset liability (OAL©) swap.

The OAL is a synthetic instrument, much like an interest rate swap. The OAL creates a means by which all competitors can help establish fair market value by triggering an obligatory swap with any institution that publishes in the firm's financial statements an unfairly high or low price for one or more of its assets or liabilities. When using the OAL, no real assets or liabilities need to change hands, which helps to preserve customer relationships; only economic results change hands. The OAL swap also allows for reasonable pricing error and transaction costs.

The characteristics of an OAL are best illustrated with examples, four of which are shown in **Table 1**. To simplify the mechanics, I have made several simplifying assumptions. First, I assume that the fair value of the asset or liability is $100. Second, the bid–ask tolerance spread is 10 percent (5 percent each way), which is extremely large for many asset types. Third, the position bite-size limit is 10 percent. Fourth, the change limit is 100 percent. These are all variables that we can think about and adjust with some experience. The four cases in Table 1 are over- and undervaluations of an asset and a liability by 25 percent, a huge amount for most assets and liabilities.

Let's start with the case of the asset overvalued by 25 percent. If management of Firm A overstates

- An appropriate time limit must be established from the report date. These obligations would last for some finite period after the financial statements are published—a month, perhaps.
- The reported fair price must be adjusted for reasonable market moves in the relevant asset classes, such as a shift in the Treasury curve.
- The obligation is voided by, say, 10 percent market event such as a market crash.
- The obligation is voided by significant name-specific news, such as a downgrade.

Other mechanics must also be worked out. For example, the accounting for the swaps could be han-

Table 1. Obligatory Asset/Liability Swap Examples

	Asset		Liability	
Item	Overvalued	Undervalued	Overvalued	Undervalued
Fair price	100	100	100	100
My reported price	125	75	125	75
OAL execution price	119	79	119	79
My exposure action for up to 10 percent of my position per SWAP executed	Increase	Decrease	Decrease	Increase
Maximum change; resulting exposure	250	0	250	0

Assumptions: Fair Price = 100.
Bid–Ask tolerance Spread = 10 percent (½ each way).
Bite-size Limit = 10 percent.
Change Limit = 100 percent.
Price Error = 25 percent.

the value of an asset on its books by 25 percent, a competitor can use the OAL to short 10 percent of the offending position to Firm A synthetically at Firm A's price less half the bid–ask spread, which turns out to be about $6 (5 percent of $125). So if Firm A says the asset is worth $125, in effect, it is forced to buy 10 percent more at $119 from the first competitor, and so on up to 10 times 10 percent. In this case, Firm A should be happy because it is buying more at a 5 percent discount from what it asserts is fair value, and the competitors who know that the true value is really $100 are happy because they are selling at a higher price. The reverse is true if an asset or liability is underpriced. This is an example of the market's disciplinary action.

Obviously, certain implementation controls are necessary:

dled individually, or better still by a clearing house.

I invite our profession to think about and work on this concept or any other concept that will enable us to view and report assets, liabilities, and surplus or net worth at values close to what they are worth in a free market. This will bring reason, fair risk assessment and comparison, and better decision making to our business.

Risk and Return on Surplus or Net Worth

The surplus or net worth of any financial intermediary is really somebody else's asset (or liability). Therefore, all of the familiar concepts of risk and return apply. The expected return on net worth or return on equity should be proportional to the risk that the net worth experiences. The actual risk of the net worth should show up in its volatility, both in the market price of that net worth and in the financial statements. If the net worth takes no risk, then the return on equity should be approximately equal to the risk-free rate.

Many of the assets and liabilities of financial intermediaries are fixed-income in nature. This is true for banks, S&Ls, and most insurance companies. Because of the predominantly fixed-income nature of the assets and liabilities, most financial intermediaries have direct exposure to interest rate risk. It is important to understand and assess the interest rate risk not only of the assets and liabilities, separately, but also of their combination—the surplus or net worth of the financial intermediary.

This is not to say that interest rate risk is the only risk to which a financial intermediary is exposed. Interest rate risk varies by type of intermediary, but it is an important risk to any financial intermediary. This means that management of interest rate risk for financial intermediaries is important.

Management of Interest Rate Risk

Duration is a useful measure of interest rate risk for assets and liabilities, and it has become a cornerstone of fixed-income management. Little is known, however, about the duration of net worth or surplus.

Duration of surplus measures the interest rate risk of the shareholders of a financial intermediary (or policyholders or depositholders of a mutual organization). Managing the interest rate risk of surplus is approximately the same as managing the duration of surplus.[2]

The derivation of the duration of surplus (D_S) begins with the accounting identity: Surplus (S) equals assets (A) minus liabilities (L). Then, because asset and liability durations are linear in the weights of the composite assets and liabilities, duration of surplus (D_s) can be defined as:

$$D_S * S = (D_A * A) - (D_L * L),$$

From this equation, it follows that:

$$D_S = D_L + (A/S) * (D_A - D_L),$$

or the duration of surplus equals the duration of the liabilities plus the product of financial leverage, as measured by the asset-to-surplus ratio (A/S) and the mismatch between asset and liability durations ($D_A - D_L$).

[2]Most of the text that follows is based on T.E. Messmore, CFA, "The Duration of Surplus," *Journal of Portfolio Management* (Winter 1990):19–22.

Because leverage is typically high in most financial intermediaries, any mismatch ($D_A - D_L$) is magnified, sometimes significantly. Take, for example, the duration of assets for an S&L in the early 1980s. Its primary assets were home mortgages, many of which were 30 years in length. The duration of a home mortgage in the late 1970s was approximately 10 years, and the duration of a savings deposit was approximately zero. (Remember how S&Ls complained when they had to get their capitalization ratios up to 3 percent, which would imply a leverage ratio of at least 33? Leverage is the reciprocal of the capitalization ratio.) Thus, the duration of surplus of the S&L industry was almost 300 years, which is a long duration. (For reference, the duration of a 30-year Treasury bond is about 10.) The S&L industry took a lot of interest rate risk.

Figure 1 provides a graphic interpretation of the relationships underlying the duration of surplus concept. The basic equation is a linear equation in the form of $y = a + bx$. By defining the x-axis to be mismatch ($D_A - D_L$), we can see that the slope of the line equals the leverage of the company, or A/S. The y-intercept equals D_L, and the x-intercept equals $-D_L/(A/S)$.

The duration of surplus equation reveals that managing the interest rate risk of a firm is a function of both asset and liability management and the corporate finance function of managing financial leverage. In my opinion, it is absolutely critical to the financial health of an organization to tie in the corporate finance or treasury function, which controls the leverage factor.

Application to Interest Rate Risk Management

Figure 1. Surplus Duration Relationships

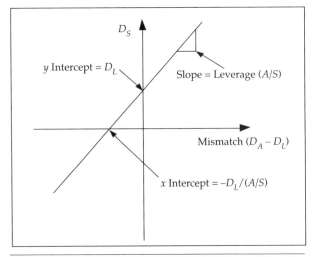

Source: Messmore, "The Duration of Surplus."

Examination of the basic relationships in the duration of surplus formula provides some interesting insights on ways to manage interest rate risk under various cases:

◼ *Perfectly matched asset and liability durations.* In this case, the duration of surplus is equal to the duration of the liabilities. The interest rate risk of surplus is not zero but is equal to D_L or D_A (which themselves are equal). Therefore matching asset and liability durations does not enable managements, accountants, and regulators to ignore interest rate risk, even though the footnotes to the financial statements assert to the contrary.

◼ *The immunizing mismatch.* One way for a financial intermediary to eliminate interest rate risk is to find the immunizing mismatch:

$$D_S = 0 = D_L + (A/S) * (D_A - D_L),$$

$$D_A - D_L = -D_L/(A/S).$$

Thus, the mismatch that creates zero duration of surplus is negative and equals minus the duration of liabilities divided by the leverage factor (A/S).

◼ *The immunizing asset duration* (D_{AZ}). Another way to eliminate interest rate risk is to find the immunizing asset duration:

$$\begin{aligned} D_{AZ} &= D_L * [1 - 1/(A/S)] \\ &= D_L * (1 - S/A) \\ &= D_L * L/A. \end{aligned}$$

Note that an increase in leverage causes the asset duration required for zero surplus duration to increase, not decrease, as most people might expect.

◼ *Negative surplus.* Here the surplus cushion form of the basic equation is most convenient to use; that is,

$$D_S = D_L + (D_A - D_L/(S/A).$$

When the cushion is negative, such as when a pension plan is underfunded, larger mismatches cause smaller D_S. A risk-averse strategy with asset duration shorter than liabilities creates a positive second term and makes surplus more, not less, volatile. This means that an underfunded pension fund can ill-afford to be short mismatched. The greater the surplus cushion, the larger mismatch risk the intermediary can assume for equivalent overall interest rate risk.

◼ *Zero surplus.* When surplus equals zero, then A = L; therefore, D_S is undefined and

$$D_S * S = (D_A * A) - (D_L * L)$$

$$D_A * A = D_L * L$$
$$D_A = D_L.$$

Nevertheless, only when surplus equals zero will a matching strategy immunize the asset/liability portfolio. Managers claiming no interest rate risk because assets and liabilities are matched are either naive or admitting they have no surplus.

Insights into the Property Casualty Industry

The duration of surplus concept provides a convenient and useful framework for comparing the apparent interest rate risk strategy of competing firms. It is also useful for analyzing whether a management understands its position and articulates a strategy consistent with its actual position with regard to duration of surplus. We applied this technique on an industrywide basis in an internal analysis of the property/casualty insurance industry. We used year-end 1987 data from 2,400 companies reported in the A.M. Best Online data base.

Table 2 shows the basic data and the durations for the industry. On an estimated market value basis, the property/casualty business at the end of 1987 had assets of $426 billion, liabilities of $266 billion, and surplus value of $160 billion. At that time, statutory book value surplus was $104 billion. GAAP net income was $13.7 billion for the year. From the Best data base (Schedule P), we estimated durations of about 5.4 for assets and about 1.9 for liabilities.

Table 2. Property/Casualty Industry Analysis, December 31, 1987

Item	Billions of Dollars	Duration
Assets (PV)	$426.0	5.4
Liabilities (PV)	266.0	1.9
Surplus (PV)	160.0	11.2
Stat. book value surplus	104.0	
GAAP net income	13.7	

Source: Estimates compiled by Travelers from AM Best On-Line data base.

The estimated mismatch (5.4 – 1.9 = 3.5) is very large, large enough to raise a question about the validity of the annual report footnotes stating how companies "generally match the maturity of their assets and liabilities." How can each of the companies be well matched when the industry in the aggregate is so mismatched?

From the formula, the values from Table 2 indicate a duration of surplus of 11.2 for the property/casualty industry $(D_S = 1.9 + (426/160) \times (5.4 - 1.9) =$

11.2). At 1987 interest rates, the duration of a 30-year Treasury bond was about 10. So the property/casualty industry, which claims to be well matched, had more interest rate risk than the long Treasury. This suggests that an equity investment in the property/casualty industry was a better, or at least a longer, interest rate play than purchasing long-term Treasury bonds. Perhaps this helps explain the old Wall Street adage that the property/casualty industry is little more than a leveraged interest rate play.

Using the duration formula, we estimated that a 1 percentage point increase in interest rates would have caused the surplus of the industry to have changed by $17.9 billion, which is more than the full year's net income for the industry. In fact, a 76 basis point increase in interest rates would have equaled the annual earnings of the industry. Because rate changes of that magnitude occur often, this indicates the business had more interest rate risk than most people thought. In some sense, duration of surplus should be more important to management than annual earnings.

The immunization equation reveals that the property/casualty industry, because of its leverage, would have to lower or shorten its duration of assets to 1.2 to eliminate its interest rate risk. Of course,

industry management would not tolerate that, but such a move would be necessary to make the footnote assertions supporting amortized-cost book value accounting treatment valid.

Conclusion

Duration of surplus is a useful concept for understanding the interest rate sensitivity of the surplus or net worth of a financial intermediary, especially one with predominantly fixed-income assets and liabilities. It provides management with useful tools and insights in managing a firm's surplus. It also gives accountants and regulators a framework within which to check whether the accounting assumptions are fairly applied.

Duration of surplus demonstrates that (1) the common understanding of immunization as matching the duration of assets and liabilities is flawed, or at least misapplied; (2) any mismatch between the assets and liabilities has a magnified effect on the surplus or net worth of the firm because of leverage; and (3) financial leverage can be used by the corporate finance function to increase and decrease the interest rate sensitivity of the firm's economic wealth.

Question and Answer Session

Thomas E. Messmore, CFA

Question: Would market value accounting, if enacted, be applauded by your peers at Travelers?

Messmore: I think it would be applauded by the investment-oriented peers and not applauded by the accountants and probably some members of management.

Question: Does the presence of cash flow justify the duration mismatch of assets and liabilities?

Messmore: Can you rely upon future income and premium cash flows to pay off expiring claims or liquidations? That is the going-concern argument, and I think some of that is legitimate.

Question: Did you include equities in your calculation of assets for the property/casualty industry?

Messmore: Yes, although equities are not a significant portion of industry assets. I think we put them in with a duration of 4, although it is possible to argue about whether 4 is too high or too low. Regardless of equity durations, the small relative equity weighting causes any error in the assumption to not change the results much.

Question: What level of mismatch would you be willing to support for the property/casualty industry?

Messmore: I believe the level of mismatch should be lower than it currently is, but it should be substantially greater than zero.

Market Value Accounting—An Idea Whose Time Has Come?

Phillip D. Parker[1]
Associate General Counsel
Securities and Exchange Commission

The Securities and Exchange Commission is urging that all investment securities held as assets by financial institutions be required to be reported at market value. Although the move would be a regulatory benefit, it nevertheless will have to overcome hurdles before it can be implemented on a comprehensive basis.

In December 1991, Congress passed what was referred to, in Washington parlance, as "a narrow banking bill." That means it was only 450 pages long. The only provision in the bill that was relevant to market value accounting did not mandate its use but merely directed the federal banking agencies to develop methods for supplemental disclosure of market values in the call reports filed with each agency. I mention the bill, however, because the crisis in our bank and thrift industries continues to provide much of the impetus for the debate about the adequacy of existing accounting standards.

The Securities and Exchange Commission formally entered this debate in September 1990, when Chairman Richard C. Breeden testified on behalf of the Commission before the Senate Banking Committee. He stated, "The Commission recognizes that transforming the accounting standards of banks and thrifts from a cost to a market-based standard is a complex undertaking, and we realize that studies are currently under way concerning these issues. The objective of these efforts should be to achieve financial reporting that uses appropriate market-based measures of valuation at the earliest possible date."

The Commission's testimony pointed to the savings and loan (S&L) crisis, as well as many of the largest bank failures, as demonstrating the inherent dangers of a reporting system for financial institutions that is premised on historical cost accounting principles. The Commission urged that serious consideration be given to a requirement that all investment securities held as assets by financial institutions be reported at market value. The Commission also observed that the relevance and credibility of bank and thrift financial statements could be enhanced by broader application of market value accounting.

I will try to describe how the Commission's position on market value accounting developed, the benefits that its adoption would provide, and the hurdles it faces.

Changing Concepts of Relevance

Just as the S&L crisis colors the current debate over accounting standards, the securities laws were passed early in the New Deal as a reaction to the speculative excesses of the prior decade. Although there was little in the way of a structured system of accounting principles at that time, the Commission decided in its earliest cases that it would not permit assets to be valued on the basis of current appraisals rather than historical cost. Commissioner Robert E. Healy, who served on the Commission from 1934 to 1946, once said, "The purpose of accounting is to account, not to present opinions of value." He held strong views on this subject and has been described as a person who believed that anything that was not original cost had to be original sin.[2]

The Commission continued for more than 40

---

[1]The Securities and Exchange Commission, as a matter of policy, disclaims any responsibility for any private publication or statement by any of its employees. The views expressed herein are those of the author and do not necessarily reflect the views of the Commission or any of the author's colleagues on the staff of the Commission.

[2]Homer Kripke, *The SEC and Corporate Disclosure: Regulation in Search of a Purpose* (New York: Harcourt Brace Jovanovich, 1979), 181.

years actively to discourage the inclusion of current asset values or of any forward-looking information, such as earnings projections, in filings with the agency. Historical costs were viewed as facts that were readily ascertainable and comparatively free from manipulation, and current values were viewed as subjective opinions that were inherently unreliable. As a general matter, the Commission's disclosure standards were designed to prevent fraud, as opposed to providing information needed for investment decisions.

One of the first signs of a policy shift occurred in 1972, when the Commission initiated rule-making proceedings to consider whether to permit earnings and revenue projections to be disclosed in Commission filings. Five years later, SEC Chairman Harold M. Williams said, "The conceptual framework project must address squarely the need for financial reporting to mirror economic reality. This does not mean that accounting based on historical costs must be discarded nor does it mean that the new methodology necessary to bring financial reporting closer to an economic picture of business operations must be agreed upon as part of the conceptual framework. On the contrary, I visualize the process of developing the reporting techniques necessary to implement the goals for the conceptual framework statement as an evolutionary process which may span many years. I do believe, however, that, if the project does not result in a framework within which financial reporting can come to grips with economic realities, then the project will bear a very heavy burden of self-justification."

After a series of false starts, the Commission issued a policy statement in 1978 that encouraged the disclosure of management projections, and it adopted a safe harbor rule covering projections in the following year. This bias in favor of forward-looking information continued throughout the 1980s, culminating in the Commission's 1989 release on disclosure requirements relating to Management's Discussion and Analysis of Financial Condition and Results of Operations (MD& A), which specifies that an issuer must disclose "known trends, demands, commitments, events or uncertainties" that are "reasonably likely to have a material effect" on the issuer's financial condition or results of operations.

This shift toward more forward-looking disclosure has consistently been rationalized as necessary to ensure that investors receive relevant information, even if that information is necessarily subjective. At the same time, however, the financial statements that such disclosures accompany continue to be rooted in objective, though often largely irrelevant, historical cost. Because the transaction-based historical cost model generally recognizes changes in value only when management exercises discretion to engage in transactions, it fails to provide information relevant to an assessment of economic value.

During the 1970s, high rates of inflation led many observers to question the continuing relevance of historical cost measurements. Attention was focused on specific issues such as oil and gas and replacement-cost accounting. Over time, the failure of generally accepted accounting principles (GAAP) to reflect economic realities has led to an increasing reliance on supplemental disclosures of information needed to protect investors from being misled by reported earnings based on historical costs.

The Thrift Crisis

A review of the S&L crisis dramatically illustrates the danger of using accounting measures that do not reflect economic realities. The problem in this industry began because thrift institutions were poorly designed financial intermediaries that were more-or-less compelled to fund long-term residential mortgage loans with short-term deposits. Because of the fundamental maturity imbalance between their long-term assets and their short-term liabilities, thrifts were inherently vulnerable to the interest rate changes that hit them in a big way beginning in the late 1970s. This was precisely the type of interest rate risk that financial statements based on GAAP tended to conceal.

Although the average cost of funds for thrifts rose from 7 percent in 1978 to just over 11 percent in 1982, the preponderance of long-term, fixed-rate mortgages in their portfolios prevented a corresponding increase in revenues. In both 1981 and 1982, the average cost of funds exceeded the average return on mortgage loans. By that time, according to several studies, the thrift industry was underwater by more than $100 billion on a market value basis.

Because GAAP failed to reflect the unrealized losses imbedded in mortgage portfolios, institutions that were economically insolvent continued to operate with the benefit of federal deposit insurance. This problem was compounded when the Federal Home Loan Bank Board lowered capital requirements and adopted a series of regulatory accounting rules that permitted thrifts to inflate their reported earnings and net worth. One rule, for example, permitted thrifts to defer losses on the sale of mortgage loans during the remaining contractual life of the loans. A second rule permitted thrifts to include what was known as "appraised equity capital"—the amount by which certain capital assets had appreciated above their book value—in the computation of regulatory net worth. In other words, the thrifts could recognize unrealized gains on assets they did not intend to sell, and defer the losses on assets they had already sold.

In 1982, Congress enacted legislation that authorized federally chartered thrifts to engage in commercial real estate and consumer lending. This was the last of the legislative and regulatory changes that transformed an industry that had been characterized by slow growth attributable to limited funds availability into an industry capable of explosive growth. There was little market discipline to control this growth because depositors protected by federal deposit insurance were indifferent to the financial health of their depository institutions. Indeed, the removal of interest rate ceilings led to the emergence of a brokered deposit industry that channeled funds to the institutions paying the highest rate of interest.

By this time, the accounting practices used in the industry had also eliminated capital adequacy requirements as a meaningful source of discipline. When maintained at an appropriate level, capital requirements provide a cushion against loss and reduce the incentive to take excessive risks. The thrift regulators, by continuing to make federal deposit insurance available to economically insolvent institutions, provided the industry with every incentive to engage in aggressive growth by speculating with taxpayer dollars. It was literally a game of "heads I win, tails the FSLIC [Federal Savings and Loan Insurance Corporation] loses." Besides causing the industry to attract more than its share of fraudulent operators, this policy led to the ruinous expansion that greatly increased the ultimate losses to the government.

Benefits of Market Value Accounting

Would market value accounting have prevented the thrift crisis? No, because the crisis resulted from a variety of economic, policy, and regulatory forces. But the use of market value accounting could have contained the damage. At a minimum, market value accounting, by reflecting the economic deterioration of the industry, would have exposed the true significance of the political and regulatory policy decisions being made throughout the 1980s.

Under the most comprehensive application of market value accounting, financial institutions would be required to reflect in their financial reports the fair market value of their assets, liabilities, and off-balance-sheet items. This would enable regulators and investors to assess more precisely the true economic value and risk exposure of a depository institution. Because banks and thrifts are thinly cap-

italized, insolvencies can occur quite rapidly during volatile times. Net worth determinations based on market values would facilitate prompt corrective action, thereby helping to ensure that undercapitalized institutions are closed in a timely manner.

The use of market value accounting would also tend to make the managers of financial institutions more accountable for their investment and business decisions. The ability to disguise bad investments by leaving them buried in the portfolio would be eliminated, and the failure to hedge appropriately against interest rate risk would be revealed. The financial statements of those institutions less effective in managing interest rate risk would reflect the volatility inherent in their business, thereby providing investors and creditors with relevant information.

Finally, the use of market value accounting would eliminate the incentive to base business decisions on accounting, rather than economic, considerations. The most notorious form of this behavior is known as "gains trading," which refers to the practice of selling assets (usually investment securities) that have risen in value while continuing to hold assets that have declined in value. Gains trading takes other forms as well. The Federal Home Loan Bank Board frankly admitted, when it adopted its rule permitting the deferral of losses on the sale of assets, that it was seeking to encourage portfolio restructuring by institutions that would not sell assets if they had to recognize a loss.

Although the benefits of market value accounting are readily apparent, its opponents argue that it depends too heavily on subjective appraisals and estimates that would necessarily undermine the reliability and comparability of financial statements. Market value accounting unquestionably raises complex valuation and auditing issues that must be resolved before any decision is made to implement it on a comprehensive basis. In particular, additional work is needed to develop reasonably accurate and verifiable valuation techniques for assets, liabilities, and off-balance-sheet commitments that do not trade in active markets. Assurance is also needed that the preparation and auditing costs associated with a comprehensive application of market value accounting do not exceed the anticipated benefits.

Although these reliability concerns are real, they should not be regarded as insurmountable. Management judgments already underlie many of the figures, such as loan loss reserves and the valuation of assets acquired in purchase business combinations, that are used in current financial statements. In addition, many institutions already use market value figures for purposes of internal management. Finally, concerns about the reliability of market value information have to be weighed against the comparative relevance of the information that would be conveyed. The question is not whether market value accounting can be as precise as historical cost, but whether responsible estimates of market values would be more useful and credible than precise measures of historical cost.

The FASB Financial Investments Project

Since May 1987, the Financial Accounting Standards Board (FASB) has been reexamining the standards for recognition and measurement of financial instruments and transactions. As part of this project, the board is assessing whether to expand the use of market value data in financial statements and related disclosures. Because of the complexity of the recognition and measurement issues, the board determined that new disclosure standards should be issued as an intermediate step in the process. The FASB proposal issued on December 31, 1990, would require all entities to disclose the market value—if practicable to estimate—of most financial instruments, both assets and liabilities on and off balance sheet.

The FASB project will mean that, at least for the near term, the disclosure of market values will supplement GAAP. This disclosure experience will operate as a kind of field test for the use of market values to measure assets and liabilities. The users of financial reports will be able to assess the quality of market value information, and the market will decide over time which type of information is most relevant.

Accounting For Investment Securities

A separate issue related to the use of market value accounting involves investment securities held by financial institutions. GAAP currently permits financial institutions to classify their holdings of investment securities into either a "trading" portfolio or an "investment" portfolio. Securities in the trading portfolio must be reported at their current market value. Securities classified as investments are carried at cost (less provision for credit losses), unless an institution can show that it lacks either the intent or the ability to hold the securities.

The accounting treatment currently accorded to investment securities is based on the rationale that fluctuations in market value are irrelevant if an institution intends to hold an instrument to maturity, when it may be redeemed at its face amount. Whether management's current intent should ever dictate future business decisions is questionable, however, because management has a continuing ob-ligation to reassess the most productive uses of its assets. Moreover, the economic environment in which financial institutions now operate has led to the use of asset/liability management strategies that undermine the presumption that investment securities will be held to maturity.

In practice, management's intent to hold the securities has proven virtually impossible for auditors and others to validate, giving rise to the "gains trading" practice I referred to earlier. This unrealistic focus on intent caused the Commission to refer to the current rules as "psychoanalytic accounting" and to urge the adoption of an alternative standard. The use of market value accounting would eliminate any incentive to sell or retain investment securities for reasons of accounting treatment rather than business utility.

In response to gains trading abuses and other concerns, the American Institute of Certified Public Accountants (AICPA) attempted to prepare and issue guidance on reporting by financial institutions for debt securities held as assets. In May 1990, the AICPA published for comment proposed rules intended to provide practical guidelines for evaluating the intent and ability of an entity to hold securities to maturity. Because the comments on this proposal were generally negative, the AICPA concluded that it should no longer continue attempts to clarify the meaning of existing guidance on the intent and ability to hold. The AICPA then requested the FASB to consider whether an objective standard, such as one based on market value measurements, would be more appropriate for the purpose of gaining consistent application. The FASB is expected to issue an exposure draft concerning the measurement of investment securities within the next few months.

Because the current value of virtually all investment securities is readily ascertainable, the subjectivity of estimates is not a concern in this area. The most relevant accounting issue is whether marking investment securities to market, while continuing to measure other assets and liabilities at historical cost or historical proceeds, could lead to volatility in reported earnings and capital that would not be indicative of the depository institution's true financial condition. This distortion could potentially result because, to the extent that depository institutions engage in hedging strategies to minimize interest rate sensitivity, a partial approach to market value accounting might require some gains and losses to be recognized while not acknowledging offsetting changes in the value of other assets, liabilities, or off-balance-sheet items.

The FASB will consider this issue as part of its current project, and it may ultimately conclude that certain "related liabilities" should be marked to market in tandem with investment securities. On the other hand, the concern that this type of partial approach to market value accounting would lead to distortion may be overstated. Because many bank and thrift liabilities reprice within one year, the divergence between their book values and market values should not be as great as that for investment securities with longer average maturities. Once again, the relevant question is not whether the use of market value accounting for investment securities would lead to financial statements that are absolutely free from distortion, but whether it would lead to financial statements that are more accurate than those used today.

Another suggestion is that market valuation of the investment portfolio may cause bank and thrift managements to reduce their holdings of government securities, thereby sacrificing liquidity and asset quality merely to avoid reporting unrealized losses. This concern should not influence the outcome, because it is not the purpose of accounting standards to motivate business decisions. Rather, the sole focus should be the relevance and materiality of the information conveyed. To the extent that such concerns are valid, the financial regulators have ample authority to require appropriate levels of portfolio liquidity to satisfy prudential concerns. Institutions that placed themselves into an illiquid condition would also be subject to market discipline.

Conclusion

Is market value accounting an idea whose time has come? In a prescriptive sense, the thrust of my remarks suggests that the answer is yes. In a descriptive sense, the answer is that time, and greater experience with the disclosure of market values, will tell. In this regard, the Commission will continue to monitor the FASB financial instruments project as it moves forward.

Whatever the outcome, these issues clearly will not diminish in importance. The decisions made during the next few years will be critical to the viability of our financial reporting system, and I urge all of you to participate in the process of making those decisions.

Question and Answer Session

Phillip D. Parker

Question: Do you think the proposed changes in accounting rules will hurt the competitiveness of U.S. financial institutions relative to international financial institutions?

Parker: The Treasury Department sent Congress a report on modernizing our financial system in January 1991. The report contains a 40-page section on market value accounting, and it cites the potential effects of market value accounting on the competitiveness of banks as a relevant policy issue. At the same time, efforts are being made on an international level to harmonize the regulations being placed on institutions in various countries. So the answer to the question depends to some extent on how successful that harmonization project is.

Question: Doesn't increased disclosure go a long way toward resolving people's concerns about the failure to reflect current market value in the financial statements?

Parker: Yes, I think disclosure does resolve a lot of the concerns, and we should work toward increased disclosure even if the next step is never taken. At the same time, Accounting Series Release No. 4 said that financial statements are financial statements and disclosure is disclosure, and the one cannot be corrected by changing the result in the other. Over time, there has been more of a divergence between the information contained in the narrative portion of a disclosure document and that contained in the financial statements. Our goal should be to cause greater convergence between disclosure requirements and accounting standards. If we believe that current market values should be disclosed because they are relevant to investors, then we should try to establish accounting rules that will permit those values to be reflected in the financial statements. Ultimately, the information that is disclosed trickles down, but a lot of people look at the bottom line and rely on ratio analysis to reach conclusions that are difficult to counteract through disclosure.

Question: Do you see any link between the tax laws and the Securities and Exchange Commission's push for market value accounting?

Parker: I am not aware that the Commission has focused on the potential tax ramifications of this issue during the past year. In the 1970s, Chairman Williams gave a series of speeches on how the effects of inflation were causing corporate earnings to look larger than their real value and how the effect of taxes on those inflated earnings were an impediment to capital formation. In that sense, market value accounting is relevant to the tax laws, but the Commission has not really focused on this relationship. I said that business decisions should be motivated by economic considerations, not accounting considerations, and taxes are clearly an economic consideration businesses will take into account.

Question: Based on input to the Commission, which constituencies oppose market value accounting?

Parker: By and large, the banking and thrift industries oppose market value accounting. Each of their trade groups has lobbied Congress and the regulators very heavily. The Treasury Department's report on modernization of the financial system had a very balanced market value accounting section, but the arguments were way over here on one side and way over there on the other, because certain financial regulators, such as the Federal Reserve Board, are very skeptical about the feasibility of market value accounting.

Question: Should analysts be concerned about the estimates and appraisals required to do market value accounting? Hasn't this been a problem for certain investment companies?

Parker: The Commission does not underestimate the difficulties of estimating the market value of certain types of securities or the potential for misuse of the appraisal process. We look at the investment company industry in general, however, as one that has worked very well.

Measuring Investment Performance in an Asset/Liability Context

David F. Babbel
Associate Professor
Wharton School, University of Pennsylvania

> If maximizing the value of owners' equity is a company goal, then the actions of managers should be judged on the basis of whether they help to promote higher firm value. The time, effort, and expense required to measure total return—and to reward performance that enhances it—should increase firm value and thus justify the expense.

Performance measurement among insurers has traditionally had an accounting, rather than firm-value, focus. This has encouraged yield-seeking behavior in investments and product design. A few years ago, I formed a group of people from academia and the investment and insurance community into a task force charged with the chore of devising a measure of investment performance suitable for use by the insurance industry. My presentation in this seminar is based on a report on the task force discussion, which I wrote with Rob Stricker and Irwin Vanderhoof ("Performance Measurement for Insurers," Goldman, Sachs & Company, October 1990). Although my remarks are set in an insurance context, the paradigm we suggest for performance measurement is applicable for other financial institutions as well.

Performance and Firm Goals

One of the basic tenets of modern financial theory is that managers should act in a manner consistent with maximizing the value of owners' equity. If this maxim is accepted as the company goal, then the actions of insurance managers and operatives should be viewed in terms of whether they help to promote higher firm value. Any benchmarks the firm uses to facilitate performance measurement must be designed in a manner that is consistent with a firm-value focus.

Theoretically, the value of owners' equity in an insurance company should be the fair market value of its assets minus its liabilities. Typically, however, the focus is on accounting statements that are based on book values rather than market values. Consequently, insurance companies have traditionally relied on yield as the primary performance measurement criterion. They have collected yield data on new investments and compared those yields with other insurers' results or against a specified passive index.

Disenchantment with the use of yield measures has been growing, however. High yields that a company achieves on new investments may merely reflect the fact that its investments have more credit risk, less liquidity, more call risk, greater foreign currency exposure, or a worse duration mismatch than those of a company showing a lower yield. Recent years have witnessed an increase in interest rate volatility; the growth of the high-yield market, in which credit quality is traded off for yield; the growth of the mortgage securities market, in which prepayment risk can be traded off for yield; and the proliferation of other new security types with complex risk/reward trade-offs.

In this environment, looking at yield on new investments alone, without adjusting for the various risks associated with each security, can be misleading. Indeed, the development of modern valuation technologies for mortgages, corporate bonds, and insurance liabilities has been motivated by the fact that yield and return are not the same thing.

Comparing portfolio yields, even among insurers with similar investment strategies and risk profiles, can also be misleading. Timing differences in insurance cash flows, in conjunction with the wide swings in interest rates experienced in recent years,

52

can result in one insurer having more money to invest when rates are high and another having more money to invest when rates are low. This results in different portfolio yields for reasons beyond an investment manager's control.

A yield focus can spawn accounting games and foster portfolio reshuffling based on book values, yet it may have very little, if anything, to do with promoting higher firm value. Increasingly, insurers are recognizing the need to adopt a performance measurement system that is compatible with the objective of increasing firm value.

Enhancing Firm Value

Within the finance domain, managers can act to increase firm value in four ways:

- Investing in projects or financial securities with positive net present values (NPVs)—that is, finding undervalued assets;
- Altering the company's financial structure;
- Altering the company's duration and convexity mismatches; and
- Outperforming the company's liabilities.

Finding Undervalued Assets

For the typical industrial firm, investing in projects or securities with positive NPVs undoubtedly has the most potential for enhancing firm value. For insurers and other financial intermediaries, however, the situation is quite different. Their comparative advantage—indeed, their *raison d'etre*—is issuing customized liabilities. Their aim is to issue these liabilities, whether in the form of property/liability insurance or life/health insurance, more cheaply than they could by raising funds in the public debt markets.

With the funds collected, they invest mostly in financial securities, not in projects with positive NPVs. Because publicly traded securities, in an efficient market, are generally assumed to trade at fair prices, their NPVs are zero. Their prices are equal to the present values of expected future cash flows, discounted at the appropriate rates to reflect their relative riskiness. Even if a manager finds a security that is underpriced, its NPV, as far as the market is concerned, remains zero until it is shown that the market is wrong; thus, buying the security will have no immediate repercussions on firm value. When the market finally is convinced of its earlier mispricing, the price will quickly adjust so that NPV returns to zero. This change in equilibrium asset price will

then have a positive effect on firm value. In practice, many portfolio managers consider their comparative advantage to be an ability to find such underpriced assets.

Investments with positive NPVs could possibly be found in the private placements market. These instruments generally have less liquidity than publicly traded securities, however, and the market charges higher yields for this illiquidity. Therefore, insurers that acquire such investments may find that their firm values do not increase as much as might be expected based on yields alone, if indeed they increase at all in the short run. Only over time will the higher yields add to firm value.

In some cases, a firm might be an active participant in undertaking a business or developing real estate property with a positive NPV. The market may recognize the attractiveness of the project and reward the firm forthwith, and this reward will show up in the firm value.

Altering Financial Structure

A center of controversy in finance theory is the impact of financial structure—leverage—on the value of a firm. Empirical evidence is largely consistent with the notion that higher leverage, at least to a point, is associated with higher stock prices. Our research into this area confirms this finding for insurers.[1] An aspect of the leverage issue that is particularly perverse with insurers is the influence of the insurance insolvency guarantee programs in most states, which protect policyholders against the consequences of insurer insolvencies. These programs, which assess responsible, healthy insurers to cover the losses of insolvent insurers, create obvious incentives for excess leverage, especially among lower tier companies.

Altering the Investment Mix

Growing evidence suggests that the market recognizes the importance of asset/liability management among insurers.[2] Our studies have shown that better-matched companies command higher stock prices relative to their economic surplus.[3] This find-

[1]David F. Babbel and Kim B. Staking, "The Market Reward for Insurers that Practice Asset/Liability Management," *Financial Institutions Research*, Goldman, Sachs & Co. (November 1989).

[2]See, for example, J. Lamm-Tennant, "The Effect of Interest Rate Changes on Common Stock Returns: An Empirical Study of Insurance Companies," Working Paper, Finance Department, Villanova University (August 1989); and T.E. Messmore, "The Duration of Surplus," *Journal of Portfolio Management* (Winter 1990):19–22.

[3]See Babbel and Staking, "The Market Reward for Insurers." The economic surplus is measured by marking to market the assets and liabilities of the company and taking the difference.

ing was particularly significant during years of highest interest rate volatility and among companies that were not precariously leveraged. Perhaps the reasons for this market premium are that the insurer has goodwill or franchise value and that a company operating with a better match between assets and liabilities is more likely to be around to capture that extra value. Indeed, we found that the better match resulted in higher relative stock prices for all but the most leveraged companies, which exhibited higher stock prices by being less well matched. The value of a mismatch to this latter group arises from the option to default (i.e., "put" the liabilities to the state), and this option increases in value as a firm's business becomes more volatile.

Outperforming the Liabilities

In addition to taking measures that can have immediate impact on the stock price or market value of owners' equity, a number of actions can be taken that will affect firm value only over time. Whenever a firm earns more on its assets than it pays on its liabilities, the excess will accrue to surplus. To the extent that these increments to surplus are greater than the required return on equity, the economic value of surplus will rise.

This increment to surplus value derives from two principal sources. The operations side may be issuing liabilities on favorable terms and through cost-efficient distribution networks. Alternatively, the investment department may be experiencing favorable returns through superior timing, selection of underpriced securities, or expert liquidity management. Sometimes these two sources of value creation work together. For example, a prolonged pattern of superior investment performance will aid the sales force in attracting additional clients on favorable terms. In such a case, part of the credit for sales should go to the investment department.

A Performance Measurement System

Actions taken by a firm using the first three abovementioned means for raising firm value, if publicly known, will tend to raise stock prices. Thus, investment performance can be measured directly by the change in stock prices, net of price movements caused by changes in the broad market and the interest rate and by industry influences. Other investment actions, such as strategic allocation of investments among broad asset classes, timing, and so forth, which are taken to outperform a firm's liabilities, take longer to evaluate. The system I will describe is designed to measure the performance of assets relative to liabilities.

The first step is to determine how the firm's liabilities have performed. Because insurance liabilities are not publicly traded, a liability benchmark must be devised based on traded securities that will mirror changes in the values of the insurance firm's liabilities. Two characteristics of a liability benchmark are of utmost importance. First, it must be based on traded securities for which an active market exists; this will allow a firm to get viable quotes on a timely basis. Second, and more important, the benchmark must behave in a manner that closely parallels the market value of the liabilities over time and under disparate economic circumstances. For example, it should exhibit duration, convexity, inflation sensitivity, and sensitivity to other broad market factors in which the firm can take an investment position similar to that of the liabilities.

Using a liquid, traded securities portfolio that mimics the liabilities allows straightforward computation of a liability total-rate-of-return index against which the performance of the assets can be measured. Outperforming this liability index ensures that the asset managers are, in fact, acting in a manner consistent with increasing the value of the firm. The composition of the liability index should be updated periodically to reflect changes, over time, in the nature of the liabilities as insurance policies age and new policies are written.

The performance measurement system we recommend would measure performance based on total rate of return, comparing the total rate of return on assets to the total rate of return on the liability benchmark. Total return is a better measure than yield because it implicitly accounts for all the risks in the portfolio.

Ideally, insurers should calculate total returns on a daily basis, as do mutual funds. In practice, however, recognizing the time, expense, and effort required, calculating returns on a monthly basis should be sufficient for insurance companies. Chaining together monthly returns allows an insurer to calculate a time-weighted rate of return over any long-term horizon. It eliminates the impact of the actual timing of insurance cash flows, which an investment manager cannot control. This allows for unbiased comparisons of performance.

A comprehensive performance measurement system will permit evaluation of performance at several levels. These are shown in **Figure 1**. The system will also allow performance attribution—the determination of ingredients contributing to relative performance.

    Level I. The first step is to characterize each of the liabilities or liability groupings issued in terms of its market characteristics—duration, convexity,

Figure 1. Performance Measurement System

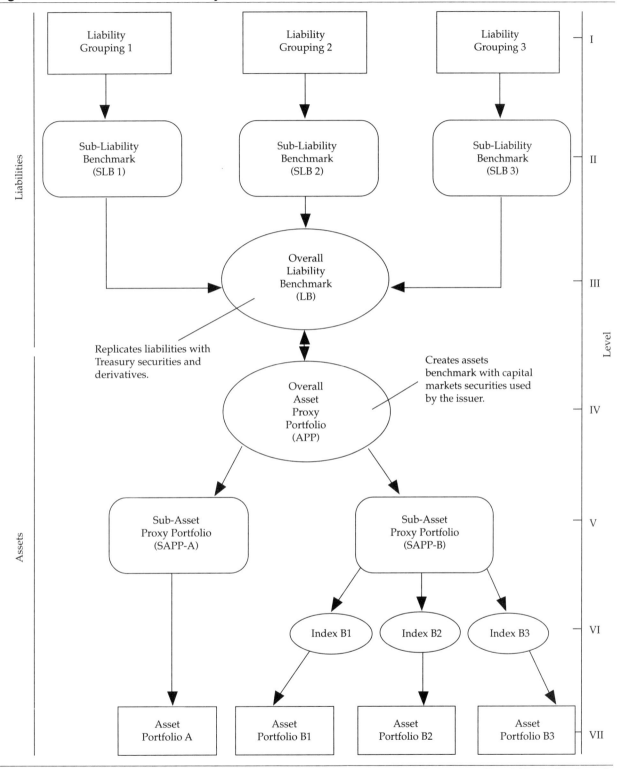

Source: David F. Babbel, Robert Stricker, and Irwin T. Vanderhoof, "Performance Measurement for Insurers," *Financial Institutions Research*, Goldman, Sachs & Co. (October 1990).

volatility, and so forth.

▦ *Level II.* Next, set up benchmark asset portfolios—sub-liability benchmarks (SLBs)—to mirror the behavior of each kind of liability. The central focus here is on the total return of the SLB at each point in time, which should mimic the total cost of the particular line of business or group of policies for which it is acting as proxy. In most cases, the liabilities can be mimicked sufficiently well by selecting from U.S. Treasury securities, their derivatives, and other liquid securities with minimal default risk.

    ■ *Level III*. The SLBs are aggregated into an overall liability benchmark (LB). The weights used in aggregating the SLBs should reflect their relative shares of the total liabilities issued; these shares are measured in market value units. The weights applied to each SLB will change over time as the proportions of business represented by each line or policy grouping change.

    ■ *Level IV*. Given the aggregate LB, the insurer can address the asset side. Here, the top-level committee charged with investment strategy defines the asset allocation and sets up an asset proxy portfolio (APP) that reflects the committee's desires regarding asset allocation and timing. To achieve target profit margins, the committee will probably include risky assets in the APP rather than limit it to just the very high-quality, liquid assets of the LB. Nonetheless, the committee's goal should be to maximize the total rate of return of the assets, subject to outperforming the liabilities. To the extent that results for the target APP differ from the LB, these investment strategists are responsible, and their decisions may be evaluated over time. For example, the APP may have more credit risk, call risk, or interest rate risk than the LB, based on their view of market conditions or bets on the economy. Making allowances for their strategic views in this process is important.

    ■ *Levels V and VI*. The APP can be divided into several smaller sub-asset proxy portfolios (SAPPs), or indexes, that could serve as benchmarks to individual portfolio or investment managers. Although each SAPP could correspond to a particular SLB, a more convenient approach might be to have the investment professionals organized according to various classes of investments (e.g., corporates, mortgages, municipals, equities, and high-yield bonds). An important characteristic of these SAPPs is that they must aggregate to the overall APP, both in investment characteristics and total rate of return. Some SAPPs may be sufficiently large that further subdivision may be convenient, providing indexes of total return on asset groupings as targets for the ultimate investment managers to achieve or outperform (e.g., Index B1, B2, and B3).

    ■ *Level VII*. The total return and risk characteristics of the investments made by the people charged with actually implementing the investment program—those who do the buying and selling of securities—must be tracked over time. Generally, their universe of permitted investments will be constrained, so their actual performance should be measured against a passive portfolio with similar investment constraints. Alternatively, their performance could be gauged against an optimized portfolio meeting the investment constraints. Appropriate constraints might include liquidity, duration, convexity, credit quality, and minimum yield requirements.

Performance Attribution

By setting up this performance measurement system in a tiered structure, as depicted in Figure 1, we have also made it easier to attribute performance correctly. At each level of performance measurement, someone is responsible for ensuring that the system operates smoothly.

    Performance attribution requires first a measure of performance so that there is something to attribute. A useful starting point is to compare the spread between the actual total rate of return on the combined investment portfolios (Level VII) and the total rate of return on the overall liability benchmark (Level III).

    This performance measure is a starting point because it measures actual investment return against a proxy for liability costs. An important step is periodically to perform economic valuations of the liabilities themselves to see whether their realized behavior has been well reflected by the asset portfolios that are used as proxies for them. If not, look for discrepancies at three levels. The first would be at Level I, where the actuaries may have improperly characterized the liabilities' investment characteristics (e.g., duration, convexity, lapse, drifts). Also, the actuaries may have correctly characterized the investment attributes of the liabilities, yet estimated poorly other attributes (e.g., mortality, frequency or severity of losses) that would produce the aberrant behavior.

    If all is well at Level I, the problem may have arisen at Level II. A financial technician may have taken the input from actuaries and incorrectly created proxy asset portfolios (liability benchmarks) intended to exhibit the same investment characteristics.

    The third step at which a problem may have arisen is at Level III, where the separate liability groupings benchmarks are weighted and combined into an overall liability benchmark. If the market value weightings of the books of business implied by the overall liability benchmark were incorrect, or evolved over time in a manner inconsistent with that assumed in the schedule for devising the benchmark, a discrepancy could exist between the actual behavior of the benchmark and the aggregate liabilities that it represents.

If the periodic examinations of the suitability of the overall liability benchmark prove satisfactory, the focus can then turn with confidence to the total-rate-of-return spread between Levels III and VII. This total spread can then be attributed to performance achieved at Levels IV, V, VI, and VII.

The committee responsible for corporate investment strategy can be evaluated on the basis of how its overall asset proxy portfolio performed relative to the overall liability benchmark. If the strategic plan is a good one, the APP over time should outperform the LB. Possibly, the strategic view is satisfactory, but the implementation is not. The people responsible for implementing the strategic view may demonstrate poor asset selection or deviate from the plan on their own recognizance. It is also possible that the strategic plan is a poor one, but the people responsible for implementing it may exceed their targets, with the result that assets outperform liabilities. This could occur at Levels V, VI, and VII.

Assuming that the SAPPs have been designed correctly, so that they aggregate to the APP, the performance of the portfolio managers can now be measured against their targets (Levels V and VI). To the extent that the portfolio managers acquire securities that differ in composition from their SAPPs or invest their available funds at different times from that assumed in the SAPPs, their performance will differ from projections.

The typical portfolio manager will have a cohort of specialists helping to acquire the investments desired on favorable terms. These specialists will be looking for undervalued assets and may exercise some discretion about the nature of assets they acquire at any time, while working over time to achieve their part of the balance the portfolio manager desires. They may be charged with investing to beat a particular index. If they outperform their target indexes, further investigation may be able to determine how this was achieved. For example, did they demonstrate superior asset selection or timing, or did they deviate from their risk norms and win their bets?

The sum of the various components of performance attribution should again equal the total-rate-of-return spread between Levels III and VII. The information collected from this endeavor will enable a fair determination of which members of the investment team contributed best toward achieving the firm's objectives and should help in readjusting investment plans for future periods. In the long run, the time, effort, and expense required to measure total return—and to reward performance that enhances it—should increase the ultimate value of the firm and thus justify the expense involved.

Asset/Liability Management Case Study

Josie McElhone
Director, Interest Rate Risk Management
Federal Home Loan Mortgage Corporation

> Freddie Mac's approach to interest rate risk management can be summed up in two words—market value. Its market value has two major components, the guarantee fee and net assets. Viewing each separately illustrates the firm's interest rate sensitivity.

Understanding the Federal Home Loan Mortgage Corporation's approach to interest rate risk management requires some understanding of the company's business. Known commonly as Freddie Mac, the company is a stockholder-owned corporation chartered by Congress. Its mission is to ensure a continuous flow of funds for housing, and to a large extent, Freddie Mac uses securitization to accomplish that mission. We buy mortgages, combine them into large groups or pools, and issue securities backed by those mortgages. The securities are passthrough securities, called mortgage participation certificates (PCs), which pay investors a *pro rata* share of the interest and principal cash flows from the mortgages. Freddie Mac guarantees payment of principal and interest on these certificates.

Freddie Mac's approach to interest rate risk management can be summed up in two words—market value. Market value accounting has been the subject of much discussion at this conference. Its proponents maintain that market value is an idea whose time has come. At Freddie Mac, market value is not just an idea; it is current practice.

Securitization Strategy

To the extent that Freddie Mac securitizes its loans, we believe that the firm bears little interest rate risk. Our objective for the past couple of years has been to securitize 95 percent of our mortgage portfolio. **Figure 1**, which shows unsecuritized mortgages as a percentage of the total portfolio, demonstrates that we have closely adhered to that target. In fact, excluding deviations caused by timing differences between mortgage purchases and security sales (the amount shown as forward sales commitments), we have been right on target during most quarters.

A natural question might be this: If securitization reduces interest rate risk, why not securitize 100 percent of the portfolio? That is simply not feasible. One reason is that the pooling process requires some mortgage inventory at all times. The retained-mortgage portfolio also includes new types of mortgage products, the volume of which is too small to warrant securitization, and other mortgages with characteristics that make securitization difficult. Finally, we maintain some mortgage inventory that is used for dollar rolls to support the Real Estate Mortgage Investment Conduit market. We consider 5 percent a reasonable amount of portfolio to maintain for these purposes, but this is a flexible target.

Claiming that securitization reduces our interest rate risk is not enough, of course. We need to be able to demonstrate that fact. We believe market value analysis provides the evidence that Freddie Mac bears little interest rate risk.

Market Value Versus GAAP

Freddie Mac estimates the fair market values of all on- and off-balance-sheet assets and liabilities every quarter. The difference between the market values for assets and liabilities is the net market value or market value of surplus.

This estimate is not a perfect measure of shareholder value. It does not, for example, include the going-concern or franchise value of the firm. Nevertheless, we believe that net market value is far superior to generally accepted accounting principles (GAAP) equity as a measure of the current economic value of the firm. To assess the firm's interest rate risk, Freddie Mac also analyzes the sensitivity of market value to changes in interest rates.

Freddie Mac has published its market value bal-

Figure 1. Unsecuritized Mortgages as a Percent of Total Portfolio

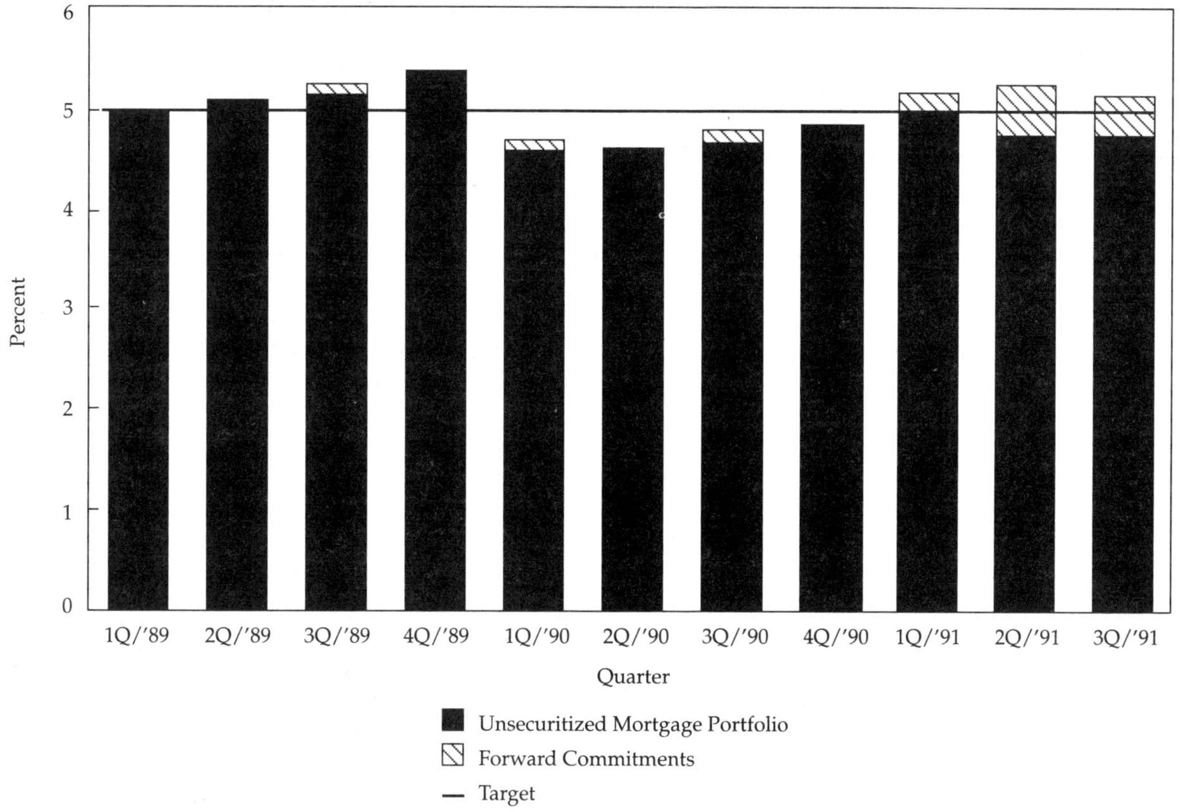

Bar chart with y-axis labeled "Percent" (0 to 6) and x-axis labeled "Quarter" showing quarters from 1Q/'89 to 3Q/'91.

Legend:
- ■ Unsecuritized Mortgage Portfolio
- ▨ Forward Commitments
- — Target

Source: Freddie Mac.

ance sheets quarterly since September 1989. We believe we are the first financial institution to publish market value information. Moreover, our market value procedures are subject to formal audit and receive a separate auditor's opinion in our financial statements.

Table 1 compares summary versions of Freddie Mac's market value and GAAP balance sheets for September 30, 1991. Mortgages are Freddie Mac's primary asset. The nonmortgage assets are primarily short-term investments with maturities of 60 days or fewer. Debt securities are both long-term debentures and short-term debt securities with durations closely matching those of the short-term assets. The subordinated debt consists primarily of zero-coupon bonds.

Notice that the market values for the on-balance-sheet assets and liabilities slightly exceed GAAP values. This is because coupons on assets and liabilities, on average, were above current market rates on this date. The market value of net assets—the difference between the values of assets and liabilities—exceeded the GAAP value by only $100 million.

When Freddie Mac securitizes mortgages, it guarantees payment on the securities in return for a fee—a specified number of basis points on the un-

paid principal balance of the mortgage, to be paid monthly. The market value balance sheet includes an estimate of the current value of these contractual fees, based on our current book of business. The major difference between the market and GAAP values of net equity is the value of this guarantee fee, an off-balance-sheet asset that is not included in the

Table 1. Comparison of Market Values and GAAP Values, September 30, 1991
(millions of dollars)

Item	GAAP	Market Value
Assets		
Net mortgages	$23,500	$24,800
Nonmortgages	20,300	19,600
	43,800	44,400
Liabilities		
Debt securities	28,800	28,900
Subordinated debt	2,700	3,100
Other liabilities	9,800	9,800
	41,300	41,800
Net asset value	2,500	2,600
Guarantee fee	—	3,700
Net equity	2,500	6,300

Source: Freddie Mac.

GAAP financial statements. We believe the GAAP statements distort reality, because the value of the guarantee fee represents a significant portion of Freddie Mac's true economic capital. In fact, as of September 30, 1991, the market value of the guarantee fee represented about 60 percent of our total market value of equity. As a result, the market value of net equity was $6.3 billion, well above the GAAP equity of $2.5 billion.

Obtaining Market Value Estimates

We use three valuation methods in constructing Freddie Mac's market value balance sheet. First, we use market quotes whenever possible—for example, in valuing our long-term debt. Second, for short-term assets and liabilities, which generally have maturities of 60 days or fewer, we use book values, because the values of these securities deviate little from par. For mortgages and for the guarantee fee, the major components of our business, reliable market prices are not available. To price these two components, we use benchmark securities and option-based pricing models.

We separate our portfolio into buckets, based on mortgage type, coupon, maturity, and seasoning. Then we select benchmark securities to help us value our portfolio. The process is analogous to determining the value of a loan by discounting its expected cash flows by the yield on a security of comparable quality. Similarly, we value our mortgages and guarantee fees by using yields on surrogate securities to discount the cash flows.

For mortgages, Freddie Mac participation certificates serve as the benchmark. These securities trade in a highly developed, liquid market; in addition, their cash flows closely mirror those of the retained mortgages.

For the guarantee fee, we use interest-only strip securities (IOs) as the benchmark. The guarantee fee functions much like an IO: It entitles the holder (Freddie Mac) to regular payments equal to a certain percent of the unpaid balance, just as an IO does.

The first step in the process is to calculate quality spreads that can be used in discounting the cash flows from the mortgages and guarantee fees. If the future payments on the loan were known with certainty, then this process would be simple. Given the price of the surrogate security, we could estimate its yield or a quality spread over the rate on a similar-maturity Treasury. Then we could use that yield, or spread, to discount the expected cash flows of a comparable-quality loan and thus determine its market value.

The process is not that simple, however, because mortgage payments are not known with certainty. Because borrowers have prepayment options, mortgage cash flows and thus values vary with each possible interest rate path. Therefore, using one interest rate scenario to project market value can be quite misleading. Instead, we use an option-based pricing model, which captures the effect of changing interest rates on market value, to estimate quality spreads for PCs and IOs. This requires estimating value under many interest rate scenarios. This methodology has become standard for valuing mortgages and mortgage securities, and the quality spreads are called option-adjusted spreads (OASs).

The OAS is defined as a constant spread that, when added to each period's risk-free interest rate, equates the expected value to the observed market price. To illustrate the concept of an OAS, consider a two-year 8 percent bond, callable in one year, and priced at $98.50. With the current rate at 8 percent, assume that the one-year Treasury rate will either rise to 10 percent or fall to 6 percent after one year, and that each event is equally likely. If rates rise, the bond will not be called after one year; if rates fall, the bond will be called. The value of the bond is determined by multiplying its value under each outcome by that outcome's probability and summing the values. Using the Treasury rates to discount the cash flows, however, produces a value above the current market price. We need to add an OAS or quality spread to each period's discount rate, as shown in the equation below, in which OAS = s:

$$\$98.50 = 0.5\left[\frac{(\$8)}{(1.08 + s)} + \frac{(\$108)}{(\$1.08 + s)(1.10 + s)}\right]$$
$$+ 0.5\left[\frac{(\$108)}{(1.08 + s)} + \frac{(\$0)}{(1.08 + s)(1.06 + s)}\right]$$

To calculate OASs for PCs and IOs, we estimate monthly cash flows along each of several hundred interest rate paths, each 360 months long. We estimate the quality spread, or OAS that, when added to each period's Treasury rate, equates the expected value of the security to the observed market price.

These OASs become inputs for valuing Freddie Mac's portfolio of retained mortgages and its guarantee fees. Using our prepayment models and interest rate process, we project cash flows for each period under each interest rate scenario. We discount those cash flows by each period's projected Treasury yield plus the OAS for the appropriate PC or IO to obtain a market value estimate for each rate path. The average value over all rate paths is the estimated market value.

Figure 2. Market Value Performance

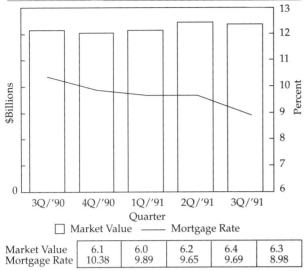

	3Q/'90	4Q/'90	1Q/'91	2Q/'91	3Q/'91
Market Value	6.1	6.0	6.2	6.4	6.3
Mortgage Rate	10.38	9.89	9.65	9.69	8.98

Source: Freddie Mac

Market Value Performance

Freddie Mac now has some history with using market values. **Figure 2** shows Freddie Mac's market value during the five quarters ending September 30, 1991. Notice that despite a decline in mortgage interest rates of approximately 150 basis points during that period, market value was remarkably stable. Freddie Mac's market value has not shown the volatility that many opponents of market value accounting contend is a major disadvantage.

Although Figure 2 demonstrates that Freddie Mac's market value has remained stable over time, it does not reveal how much of the change in value over any period of time is attributable to changes in interest rates and how much to other factors. To get a handle on that, we produce a transition analysis that estimates each component's contribution to market value. The impact of interest rate and price changes is estimated by recalculating the previous quarter's book of business at current interest rates and prices. The difference between that estimate and last

Table 2. Market Value Transition Analysis
(millions of dollars)

	Market Value 6/30/91	Rate/Price Impact	Operations Impact	Value 9/30/91
Net asset value	$2,300	$270	$ 50	$2,620
Guarantee fees	4,140	−500	90	3,730
Total	6,440	−230	140	6,350

Source: Freddie Mac.

quarter's market value is a measure of the interest rate/price impact. The operations impact is the change in market value over the quarter, holding interest rates and prices constant. It is an indicator of operational performance during the quarter.

Table 2 shows the transition analysis for the quarter ended September 30, 1991. That quarter was marked by a substantial decline in interest rates, which produced an abnormally large rate/price impact of $230 million. During 1990, for example, interest rate changes affected market value by less than 3 percent.

We find this analysis useful because it gives us a feel for each component's contribution to market value. It gives us a measure of interest rate sensitivity in past periods. To measure interest rate risk, however, we need a forward-looking measure as well.

Measuring Interest Rate Risk

Interest rate risk means different things to different firms. In general, it is the risk that changes in interest rates will adversely affect the firm, as measured by the sensitivity of some target variable to interest rates. That target variable can be market value, net income, or some other measure.

The appropriate strategy for controlling interest rate risk can differ dramatically depending on the target variable chosen. To illustrate, **Figure 3** shows this difference for a firm with 10-year assets and 3-year liabilities, currently earning a fixed spread of $2.7 million. If that firm's target is net interest margin over a horizon of three years or less, then it appears to have no interest rate risk: Net income is constant as interest rates change. If, on the other

Figure 3. Market Value versus Net Income

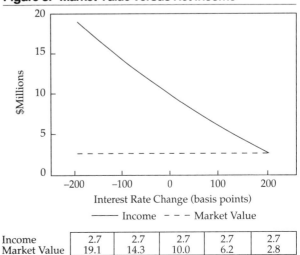

Income	2.7	2.7	2.7	2.7	2.7
Market Value	19.1	14.3	10.0	6.2	2.8

hand, market value is the target variable, the firm has considerable interest rate risk. With its long-term assets and short-term liabilities, the firm's market value declines sharply as interest rates rise.

Freddie Mac's primary target variable is market value. We believe market value is the best measure of interest rate risk because it takes into account all future cash flows from the current book of business. Therefore, it is a leading indicator of future earnings, but its performance does not depend on the choice of an arbitrary time horizon.

Freddie Mac's objective is to minimize the sensitivity of market value to changes in interest rates. This means more than simply duration matching. The market value of a duration-matched firm is insensitive, but only for small changes in interest rates. If the convexities of assets and liabilities differ substantially, as in the example shown in **Figure 4**, market value can be sensitive to even moderate rate changes.

Freddie Mac believes that matching both duration and convexity of assets and liabilities is important. **Figure 5** illustrates the sensitivity of net market value for the firm for which only duration is matched. In contrast, successfully matching both duration and convexity produces a relatively stable market value over a wide range of interest rates.

Freddie Mac's Interest Rate Sensitivity

Freddie Mac's market value can be viewed as having two major components: the guarantee fee and net assets. Viewing each component separately helps to understand the firm's interest rate sensitivity.

Guarantee Fees

The value of Freddie Mac's guarantee fee under different interest rate environments is shown in **Fig-**

Figure 4. Market Value Sensitivity of Assets and Liabilities, Duration-Matched Firm

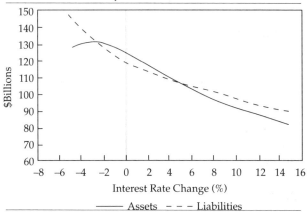

ure 6. Guarantee fee value tends to rise and fall with interest rates. As interest rates fall, mortgage loans prepay, which curtails the guarantee fee stream from the current book of business and thus reduces its market value. As interest rates rise, prepayments slow and the guarantee fee stream lasts longer, increasing its market value.

This analysis does not provide a complete picture, however, because Freddie Mac can expect to receive a share of refinanced loans that result for prepayments. Therefore, we include expected replacement business in the analysis by making a simple assumption: that prepayments are replaced with new loans of equal principal, and that Freddie Mac earns a fixed profit spread on those new loans. These assumptions are used in developing the replacement curve shown in Figure 6. Combining the two curves—guarantee fee plus replacement—gives us an estimate of the interest rate sensitivity of Freddie Mac's guarantee fees. That this curve is relatively flat is additional evidence that securitization limits our interest rate risk.

Figure 5. Market Value Sensitivity—Duration Matching versus Duration and Convexity Matching

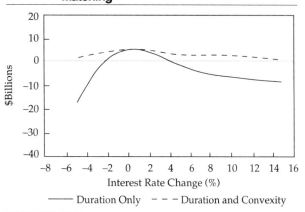

Figure 6. Sensitivity of Guarantee Fees to Interest Rates, September 30, 1991

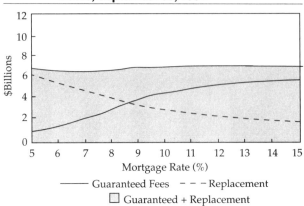

Source: Freddie Mac.

Net Assets

The other major component of Freddie Mac's market value is net assets, consisting primarily of mortgage assets financed by debt. Currently, about half the funding is long-term debt and the rest is short-term debt. This short funding produces some interest rate sensitivity for net assets, as illustrated in **Figure 7**. Net assets, however, represent a relatively small share of Freddie Mac's total market value plus replacement. To the extent that we issue more long-term debt, including callable debt, the net asset curve will become flatter over time.

Current Book of Business

Putting these curves together gives us a measure of Freddie Mac's overall interest rate sensitivity. **Figure 8** is our estimate of the interest rate sensitivity of Freddie Mac's current book of business plus replacement under various interest rate shocks. Market value remains fairly stable, particularly for lower interest rates, but even if the mortgage interest rate suddenly jumped 400 basis points to 13 percent, market value with replacement would drop by only 18 percent.

This analysis is comforting, but are we fooling ourselves? The results depend critically on the validity of the models used to obtain them, and those models require many assumptions. For example, we must make assumptions about interest rate volatility and prepayment speeds. Moreover, the starting point for the analysis is the current yield curve, and different yield curve shapes can produce different results. These factors can be classified as "model risk." To assess their importance, we conduct a variety of sensitivity analyses to determine how changing assumptions affects our results. Thus far, our results appear stable over a wide range of assump-

tions, but we are constantly working to improve our models and the assumptions we use.

A New Approach to Risk Measurement

Although we find interest rate sensitivity curves, such as those shown in Figure 8, useful risk profiles, they have some defects. First, they do not really provide interest rate measures. They do not tell us whether Freddie Mac has too much or too little interest rate risk. Second, the analysis assumes that the yield curve shifts instantaneously by as much as several hundred basis points, which is not realistic. Rather than instantaneous jumps, interest rates tend to evolve slowly.

In light of these problems, we have been experimenting with a new approach to measuring interest rate risk. Our current estimate of market value is the mean of several hundred market values, one for each rate path that we run. Along each rate path, interest rates evolve slowly, rising and falling over a period of 360 months. The frequency distribution of those market values can be used as the basis for a new measure of interest rate risk. For example, **Figure 9** shows the frequency distribution of market value with replacement as of September 30, 1991. These frequencies can be treated as probabilities; thus, if 70 percent of the rate paths produce market value with replacement above $9 billion, then the probability that the true market value exceeds $9 billion is assumed to be 70 percent. This framework lends itself to establishing risk thresholds or constraints. For example, the goal might be to ensure that true market value is not more than 10 percent below the current estimate. We can use this analysis to determine the probability that we meet that requirement.

Figure 7. Sensitivity of Net Assets to Interest Rates, September 30, 1991

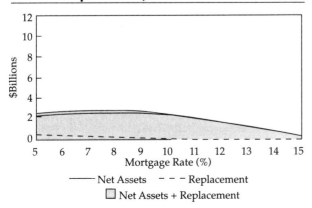

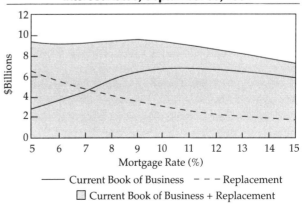

Figure 8. Sensitivity of Current Book of Business to Interest Rates, September 30, 1991

Source: Freddie Mac.

Source: Freddie Mac.

Figure 9. Market Value with Replacement—Frequency Distribution, September 30, 1991

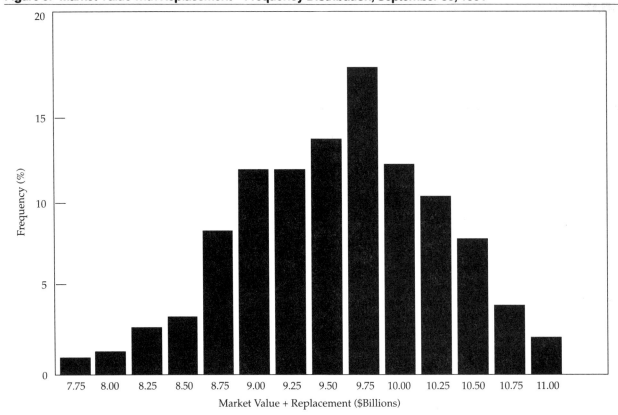

Market Value + Replacement ($Billions)

Source: Freddie Mac.

Summary

Freddie Mac takes market value analysis seriously. In fact, the firm sets market value targets that are used as one determinant of incentive pay. We regularly present market value estimates and sensitivity analysis to our board and to senior management as performance indicators and interest rate sensitivity measures. We discuss market value with equity analysts, and we believe that their interest and understanding of this concept is growing.

Congress and financial institution regulators are beginning to take market value analysis seriously as well. For example, the Department of Housing and Urban Development (HUD), which regulates Freddie Mac and the Federal National Mortgage Association (Fannie Mae), requires both firms to conduct a market value analysis once a year. HUD also looks at market value as a measure of our interest rate risk. During the past couple of years, various agencies—including the Treasury Department, the Congressional Budget Office, and the General Accounting Office—have examined Freddie Mac and Fannie Mae to determine the government's risk exposure. Each of those agencies has been very interested in market value and its usefulness as a measure of interest rate sensitivity.

We believe that awareness of market value is growing. Financial institution regulators, particularly those charged with thrift supervision, seem to have adopted the idea that market value analysis is the way to go. Thrift Bulletin 13 requires all thrifts to estimate the market value of equity and to set interest rate objectives related to how much market value would change if interest rates rose or fell. The Office of Thrift Supervision also has proposed an interest rate risk component of the risk-based capital regulations that incorporates the market value of equity concept.

Although it will take time, I believe that market value accounting is coming. The first major step will come this year, when the Financial Accounting Standards Board (FASB) puts into place requirements for market value disclosures for all financial instruments.

Question and Answer Session

Josie McElhone

Question: Do your market value estimates account for the credit risk of your large contingent liability (i.e., the guarantee of principal and interest)?

McElhone: They do, but we are not entirely satisfied with our procedure yet. In the market value balance sheet, we use the book value of loan loss reserves as a proxy for credit risk. We do that for a couple of reasons. One is that we are essentially the only institution doing market value analysis, and we do not want to confuse the market. The appropriate measure for credit risk is the expected present value of future default costs from our book of business. That is a different concept from loan loss reserves, and it is likely to be a somewhat different number. Given the market's unfamiliarity with market value concepts generally, we were concerned that using one measure of credit risk on the market value balance sheet and another on the GAAP balance sheet would be unnecessarily confusing. We hope that FASB will provide some guidance on this issue when it comes forward with its market value disclosures.

In addition, our financial research department has a model incorporating stress-test types of analysis that we use regularly to estimate the present value of future default costs on our book of business. Similar to our market value models, the default cost model uses a Monte Carlo-type analysis that projects interest rates under different environments and estimates defaults and default costs under each of those environments. The average of costs under all of those scenarios is the expected present value of default costs. Our tests indicate that this value typically has been fairly close to the value of loan loss reserves on our balance sheet. This has given us some comfort that the measure we are using is not too far off. Credit risk is a very important issue in going to full market value accounting.

Question: Congress has been debating capital standards for Freddie Mac. What type of capital requirement is likely to be established?

McElhone: The current proposal for Freddie Mac's risk-based capital would apply a stress-test analysis using a 10-year depression at least as severe as the one that occurred in Texas during the 1980s. The risk-based capital requirement would be that Freddie Mac had to survive that 10-year period. At the same time, we would have to survive certain specified interest rate risk tests. The House approved a bill that would set our risk-based cap-ital requirement according to this method, and the Senate is close to approving one.

Question: Do you estimate the duration of your surplus?

McElhone: We periodically estimate the duration of our equity and of our assets and liabilities, including our off-balance-sheet guarantee fees. We do not focus on duration, however, because it only tells you sensitivity over a relatively small range of interest rates. Instead, we look at our interest rate profile over a wide range of rates.

Question: Since you have adopted the market value approach, are your strategies in managing the firm decidedly different from what they were before?

McElhone: Freddie Mac has traditionally had a long-term focus, even before it began estimating market value. That is not to say we totally ignore earnings. We are concerned about earnings sensitivity—as are our board, shareholders, and equity analysts—but we focus more on market value, which is the long-term value of the firm. We believe that focusing exclusively on short-term earnings can cause a firm to make decisions contrary to its long-term best interest.

Self-Evaluation Examination

1. For asset/liability portfolios, the risk-free asset is:
    a. T-bills.
    b. A Treasury bond that matches the duration of liabilities.
    c. An immunized portfolio matched to the liabilities.

2. Leibowitz's asset/liability model suggests that increasing the duration of the bond portfolio may justify an increased allocation to equities.
    a. True.
    b. False.

3. Leibowitz further argues that for pension plans, limiting surplus loss is a more important shortfall constraint than limiting asset value loss.
    a. True.
    b. False.

4. According to Fong, changes in volatility should be explicitly considered in the overall risk control of the portfolio.
    a. True.
    b. False.

5. Because convexity of liabilities cannot be calculated, it should not be considered in asset/liability management.
    a. True.
    b. False.

6. Weinberger argues that an asset/liability model should consider the correlation of both assets and liabilities to:
    a. GNP.
    b. Inflation.
    c. Interest rate.
    d. All of the above.

7. Weinberger notes that one problem of current asset/liability models is that they are static rather than dynamic and, therefore, fail to consider future premium flows and the benefit of franchise value.
    a. True.
    b. False.

8. According to Gibson, which of the following is not a way to manage liabilities:
    a. Persistency bonuses.
    b. Cutting expenses.
    c. Interest-crediting strategies.
    d. None of the above.

9. Universal life insurance policies offer the policyholder an opportunity to antiselect against the company.
    a. True.
    b. False.

10. Asset/liability modeling is important for (1) risk analysis, (2) evaluating interest crediting strategies, (3) merger and acquisition work.
    a. 1 and 2.
    b. 1 and 3.
    c. 2 and 3.
    d. 1, 2, and 3.

11. When modeling assets and liabilities, it is important to consider several different interest rate scenarios.
    a. True.
    b. False.

12. The duration of surplus is equal to the duration of assets minus the duration of liabilities.
    a. True.
    b. False.

13. According to Messmore, book value accounting systematically understates:
   a. Risk.
   b. Return.
   c. Net worth.

14. Messmore estimates that the duration of surplus for the property/casualty business at the end of 1987 was:
   a. 1.9 years.
   b. 5.4 years.
   c. 11.2 years.

15. According to Parker, the advantages of market value accounting are that it:
   a. Provides a means to evaluate political and regulatory policy decisions.
   b. Provides accountability of managers.
   c. Eliminates incentives to base decisions on accounting rather than economic considerations.
   d. All of the above.

16. Because GAAP accounting fails to reflect unrealized losses imbedded in mortgage portfolios, economically insolvent institutions were able to continue to operate.
   a. True.
   b. False.

17. Babbel argues that total return is a superior performance measurement to yield because it implicitly accounts for all the risks in the portfolio.
   a. True.
   b. False.

18. Performance measurement can only address asset returns and, therefore, only serves investment interests. Consequently, net yield spread is a more appropriate way to evaluate asset/liability portfolios.
   a. True.
   b. False.

19. Since Freddie Mac adopted market value accounting for its assets and liabilities, McElhone observes that the volatility of its market value has increased dramatically.
   a. True.
   b. False.

20. In its financial statements, Freddie Mac uses which of the following valuation methods:
   a. Book value accounting.
   b. Market value accounting.
   c. Benchmark securities and options-based pricing.
   d. None of the above.
   e. Some combination of all of the above.

Self-Evaluation Answers

1. c. See Leibowitz, page 7.
2. a. See Leibowitz, page 10.
3. b. See Leibowitz.
4. a. See Fong, page 15.
5. b. See Fong.
6. d. See Weinberger, page 24.
7. a. See Weinberger.
8. b. See Gibson, page 32.
9. a. See Gibson, pages 30–31.
10. d. See Matczak, page 33.

11. a. See Matczak, page 35.
12. b. See Messmore, page 42.
13. a. See Messmore, page 39.
14. c. See Messmore, page 43.
15. d. See Parker, page 48.
16. a. See Parker, page 47.
17. a. See Babbel, page 54.
18. b. See Babbel, page 54.
19. b. See McElhone, page 61.
20. e. See McElhone, pages 59–60.

Order Form

Additional copies of *Managing Asset/Liability Portfolios* (and other AIMR publications listed on page 72) are available for purchase. The price is **$20 each in U.S. dollars**. Simply complete this form and return it via mail or fax to:

AIMR
Publications Sales Department
P.O. Box 7947
Charlottesville, Va. 22906
Telephone: 804/980-3647
Fax: 804/977-0350

Name _____

Company _____

Address _____

_____Suite/Floor _____

City _____

State _____ZIP _____

Daytime Telephone _____

Title of Publication	**Price**	**Qty.**	**Total**
_____	_____	_____	_____
_____	_____	_____	_____

Shipping/Handling	
❏ All U.S. orders:	Included in price of book
❏ Air mail, Canada and Mexico:	$5 per book
❏ Surface mail, Canada and Mexico:	$3 per book
❏ Air mail, all other countries:	$8 per book
❏ Surface mail, all other countries:	$6 per book
Discounts	
❏ Students, professors, university libraries:	25%
❏ CFA candidates (ID #_____):	25%
❏ Retired members (ID #_____):	25%
❏ Volume orders (50+ books of same title):	40%

Discount $-_____

4.5% sales tax
(Virginia residents) $ _____

7% GST
(Canada residents, #124134602) $ _____

Shipping/handling $ _____

Total cost of order $ _____

❏ Check or money order enclosed payable to **AIMR**   ❏ Invoice me
Charge to: ❏ VISA   ❏ MASTERCARD   ❏ AMERICAN EXPRESS

Card Number:_____   ❏ Corporate ❏ Personal

Signature:_____   Expiration date: _____

Selected AIMR Publications